Sonia Blandford's
MASTERCLASS

To my mother, Pauline, whose weekly reading and commentary with May came as a welcome surprise.

Sonia Blandford's
MASTERCLASS

Sonia Blandford

Paul Chapman Publishing

Paul Chapman Publishing
A SAGE Publications Company
1 Oliver's Yard
55 City Road
London EC1Y 1SP

SAGE Publications Inc
2455 Teller Road
Thousand Oaks, California 91320

SAGE Publications India Pvt Ltd
B-42, Panchsheel Enclave
Post Box 4109
New Delhi 110 017

Library of Congress Control Number: 2005903421

A catalogue record for this book is available from the British Library

ISBN 1-4129-1862-6
ISBN 1-4129-1863-4 (pbk)

Typeset by Pantek Arts Ltd, Maidstone, Kent
Printed on paper from sustainable resources
Printed in Great Britain by Cromwell Press, Trowbridge, Wiltshire

Contents

Acknowledgements   ix
Author's details   xi
Introduction   xiii

1 Masterclass   1
  Introduction   1
  Importance of looking after the individual in a community
  of learners   1
  What makes a good learning environment?   3
  Summary   5

2 Issues in education   6
  Introduction   6
  A palatable alternative to selling crisps in school tuck shops   7
  Inclusion is about identifying and removing injustices   8
  Time to give SENCOs the support they deserve   10
  Schools are a microcosm of their local community   12
  Good practice is what makes teaching a job worth having   14
  Importance of planning   16
  Noise control – a level of distraction   18
  Summary   20

3 Leadership   21
  Introduction   21
  Time for individual needs to take priority   22
  All teachers can be managers and leaders   24
  A team doesn't pull together without effective leadership   26

No teacher is an island – they need to collaborate 28

Meetings are not a waste of teachers' time 30

Teachers should seize the chance to become budget holders 32

Summary 34

4 Classroom practice 36

Introduction 36

Pupils thrive in structured, creative mess 37

Learning should be staged like scaffolding with the next level visible 39

Threats quash bad behaviour but positive reinforcement has lasting effect 41

Successful teachers focus on learning not behaviour management 43

The referee in the classroom – expectations and rules 45

Rewards and praise work much better than threats and punishment 47

Communication in schools should be in a quiet way and shouting is outlawed 49

Children who have not learnt how to behave need expert help 51

Good teachers focus on what each pupil can do 53

Assessment should be a means to improve teaching 55

The art of report writing 57

The public examination system is a bit like a lift 59

A stressed teacher will be less effective than a relaxed one 61

Summary 63

5 Arts 64

Introduction 64

A different tune 64

Teachers can still make performers of their students 68

A few tips on how to face the music of the school performance 70

Creative ideas can be found in the oddest places 72

Summary 74

6 **Professional development** 75

Introduction 75

Trainee teachers need qualified and devoted mentors 75

How to give newly qualified teachers a good start 78

Much more thought should be given to planning staff training days 80

Make provision for continuing professional development – a space to grow 82

Everyone should consider further study for themselves 84

Summary 86

7 **Futures** 87

Introduction 87

Differences in educational provision in schools and FE colleges 88

Recruit people to the profession 90

Increased use of computers has had a limited impact on learning 92

Is remodelling the National Curriculum the way forward? 94

Remodelling the workforce – how to make best use of extra staff 96

A new curriculum geared to individual needs 98

Summary 100

References 103

Index 107

Acknowledgements

Much of what is reported in each column has been observed in classrooms across Europe. To all practitioners, my thanks and appreciation for your dedication and commitment to learners of all ages.

The Masterclass columns would not have been written without the invitation and subsequent encouragement of Will Woodward, Education Editor of the *Guardian*, an experience that has been enjoyable and rewarding. Further thanks to my colleagues at Canterbury Christ Church University, particularly Dr Viv Wilson for advice and editing and to Sue Soan for proofreading. My thanks to Charlie Eldridge for his support and assistance with preparing the text.

Finally my thanks to Jude Bowen, Senior Commissioning Editor, for her encouragement in the development of this book.

Author's details

Professor Sonia Blandford is Dean of Education at Canterbury Christ Church University, which is one of the largest providers of initial teacher training and continuing professional development in the United Kingdom. Following a successful career as a teacher in primary and secondary schools, Sonia has worked in higher education for ten years. She has been an education consultant to Ministries of Education in Eastern Europe, South America, South Africa and also to the European Commission. In the UK, Sonia has worked as an advisor to LEAs and schools and co-leads the Teach First initiative. As an author of a range of education management and special needs texts, Sonia has a reputation for her straightforward approach to difficult issues. She writes in an accessible style, communicating ideas in a pragmatic manner as illustrated in *Masterclass* and her columns written for the *Guardian*.

Introduction

The opportunity to write *Masterclass* began with a phone call to the Faculty of Education. Given a hectic summer of press involvement with Teach First and the National Association of Gifted and Talented Youth Summer School, it was not unusual for local and national editors to make contact. A few days later, Will Woodward, *Education Guardian* Editor, proposed the possibility of writing a weekly column for teachers and lecturers that would inform their practice while engaging with current issues.

The *Education Guardian* had been reformatted with a new feel and the directive for my column was to explore a variety of issues in a light-hearted way with a central tenet that readers would feel confident with the comments or advice given. Readers' responses were gratefully received; mostly these were positive but some felt particular columns appeared to criticise (though this had never been the intention). Many responses welcomed the common-sense, down-to-earth approach that mirrored real events in practitioners' lives; these comments were echoed by colleagues and friends who found the columns relevant and amusing. Cliff Allen (Higher Education Academy), Mary Stiasny (Head of Education, British Council), Hugh Baldry (Teacher Training Agency) and Margaret Wallis (Director of the University Centre Hastings) are representative of the range of educationalists who were among the column's regular readership.

The intention of this book is for readers to reflect on their own practice and that of others. The majority of the columns are not time bound but address core issues that have and will continue to inform learning and teaching across all phases of education. Throughout the book, readers are encouraged to look to the future while being informed by the past. Under a broad heading, each chapter guides readers through a particular topic with an introduction that relates the chapter's content to practice. Summaries entitled 'Questions for discussion' provide reflective questions while interrogating the individual practitioner's experience.

I believe that leaders, practitioners and educators will value a moment's reflection on how a mix of places and people can provide environments in which all can learn as practice without theory is just a performance. Most of the columns draw on personal experience that occurred at the time of writing and as such provide an opportunity for readers to reflect on how the everyday can inform and stimulate educational practice. Hopefully, this collection of columns will convey the pleasure and fulfilment of teaching. Focusing on the practice of learning and teaching (pedagogy), the book creates an ethos of teaching that is celebrated in practice. While looking at the past and the present, many columns will provide a platform for the future. Though methods and theories are mentioned, readers are encouraged to develop their own framework for practice that will take them beyond established texts: to look to the future, to challenge and excite and to participate in their own Masterclass.

Questions for discussion

1. Consider how each chapter can be used as a basis for professional development.
2. Develop each question and issue by applying the ideas to your own context.
3. Share and discuss the ideas with others – challenge and excite your school or college.
4. Create your own Masterclass.

Chapter 1 provides an introduction to *Masterclass* encompassing the notion that all members of schools, colleges and higher education institutions are learners. To engage with learning is central to education, therefore every teacher has the task of instilling a passion for learning in all those who participate in their class regardless of gender, age or social, ethnic, cultural or economic background.

Readers might reflect on their own ability to learn from theory and practice; lifelong learning is a principle that enhances teachers as practitioners. The two columns provide a stimulus for practice that could generate principles for each learning community.

Chapter 2 addresses a number of issues in education: teaching; the creation of consistent policies; schools and colleges as communities; and the importance of planning. The columns are written for teachers and those who work alongside them. In every sense, a teacher is a pedagogue: a professional who practises learning and teaching.

I believe that a holistic approach to learning is the most appropriate and inclusive as described in *Every Child Matters* (DfES, 2004b). What learners experience in their place of learning extends beyond the classroom to interactions with others encountered throughout their lives (Street, 2005). Of equal importance is a sense of place – of placing the school within the community. As the government agenda continues its progress towards multi-agency community schools, a range of facilities including health, welfare and education with the school as a place of learning is paramount (DfES, 2004b). Underpinning this agenda is the ideology of inclusion so that all members of the community are able to access learning.

Chapter 3 focuses on leadership – a term that seems to have replaced management and administration. Most readers would agree that there is more than one leader within a learning community (Thomas and McNulty, 2004). Effective leadership is evident if the leader(s) knows when it is appropriate to hand over to those with greater expertise. Jazz players are well-rehearsed in such practice: individuals pass the sound from one performer to the next as the sense of the music dictates. Reference to teams is made on more than one occasion in the context of leadership, particularly those who come together to generate the best performance. This is similar to conductors of larger ensembles who are able to direct each section or player to lead in a performance as determined by the interpretation of a composer's score.

Chapter 4 concentrates on classroom practice. Much has been written in the secular and educational press about behaviour management being at the core of active learning. At Canterbury Christ Church University, Professor Janet Tod and colleagues have developed the concept of Behaviour for Learning, which I endorse within these columns (Powell and Tod, 2004).

Vygotsky (1962) is one of many theorists whose thinking has informed and prepared the way we teach. His concept of scaffolding learning has underpinned curriculum and assessment throughout the last 50 years. Educationalists and practitioners might question the relevance of such theories to the classrooms of the future, when technology will feature more predominantly in the process and delivery of learning (TES, 2005), yet behaviour management and engagement with learning remain fundamental issues in schools and colleges.

All learners in being included in education participate in assessment. Assessment for learning is a recurring theme, as various columns show how clarity of direction, instruction and engagement with the purpose and function of assessment will assist the learner.

When learners are assessed, it is their teachers who are accountable for perceived levels of achievement. This is one of the many factors that make teaching a stressful profession. Practitioners are professionals who are often advised on the need to remain calm. As the final column recommends – be a turtle and lead a balanced, healthy life! (*The Teacher*, 2005).

Chapter 5 brings together a selection of writings that relate to the curriculum. As a music teacher, music dominates the columns, for which I make no apology. Much can be learnt from one area of the curriculum and applied to another; purists may disagree. Confidence to discuss and reflect on practice within a subject is a notion that transcends any perceived differences in pedagogy.

Chapter 6 on professional development is at the heart of my own educational philosophy. I believe that engagement as a learner facilitates effective teaching. Teachers who are limited in their own learning are in danger of being limited in their teaching. In this chapter, many aspects of professional development are explored.

Leaders are taken to task on the importance of managing professional development in their schools, as are those teachers whose ability to engage in learning stops when and where they gained their qualifications. Fortunately, these are few in number and the teaching profession is largely one of committed professionals who welcome the opportunity to engage in professional development on a regular and informed basis.

Chapter 7 considers the future of schools and colleges. For schools there is an opportunity to create a new workforce. The challenge is to create a balance between recruiting and retaining teachers while accommodating the 22 aspects of the remodelling agenda (DfES, 2003a). Workforce reform is prevalent within the public sector and the government's agenda is influencing every aspect of our practice (DfES, 2002).

The North American model of community schooling is becoming commonplace in the UK as schools and colleges become the location of community resources for education, health and welfare. Multi-agency working will provide the framework for our future practice as qualified and unqualified practitioners work together to provide an environment for learning. The impetus for change is ideological; the outcome is a set of policies, supported by government, unions, school and college leaders and a wide range of agencies, that have gathered momentum and focus on the child and other learners.

1 Masterclass

Introduction

As a practitioner or learner, your reason for reading *Masterclass* might be to enhance your understanding of learning and teaching. As a parent or guardian, it might be to develop your understanding of schools and colleges. Whatever your motivation, all stakeholders will recognise that education plays a powerful part in developing society. Schools and colleges are places where the core business of each day is learning and teaching.

Masterclass began with the story of Joe, who so wanted to learn and was encouraged to find his own way supported by committed practitioners. Teachers took his ideas and provided the means to inform and develop Joe as an individual learner, so that he discovered learning.

It is axiomatic that the environment in which learning takes place impacts on all of its learners. The second column describes what I consider to be a failed enterprise in the development of a place of learning. Not all public private initiatives need to be so ineffective; however, such partnerships are dependent on a balance between public and private sectors – does one player enhance the other? Critically, can educationalists use their expertise to inform the architects of the environments in which they work?

Importance of looking after the individual in a community of learners

Joe loved the stars. Every night he gazed through his telescope towards the sky, learning about the Plough and the Milky Way with the greatest of ease. However, in school he just plodded, until one day in the science lesson the teacher asked, 'Who can recognise the Milky Way?' Joe was so animated in his response that the class felt as if they were looking through the telescope with him. A project followed, led by Joe that resulted in a special edition of the school magazine. This magical engagement with learning eventually led Joe to progress to higher education (the first in his family) and onto a job with a well-known research company.

The Joes of this world are in our classrooms and staffrooms. The message here is: is there a way that as teachers we can unlock that enthusiasm and commitment to learning? There are many examples of primary and secondary schools that have inspired pupils to learn through an activity not normally found in the curriculum: bands, football, bird watching … the list is endless.

Through my career I have witnessed good, bad and indifferent pupils being taught in such a way that they engaged with learning – playing a note on an instrument, catching a ball – which helped them with the fundamentals of reading and writing.

We know the task of teachers is to engage learners. An ability to teach stems from a combination of personality, knowledge and communication skills. Variety with a consistency of expectations is the key. It is important to think beyond the class to the individual. Teachers should ask themselves: what in the lesson will make the learners' eyes sparkle?

As a community of learners, we can get to know the individual in our classroom, to build on their success and to transfer skills to other areas of the curriculum. That is the magic of learning, and the magic of teaching. At the beginning of each lesson, teachers need to be precise in what they want each pupil to learn; the aim by the end of the lesson is that this has been achieved. They will feel good, as will the pupil.

Teachers should not try to 'eat the elephant whole'. With any skill, concept or facts, they should build towards the pupil, grasping the elements until eventually the scaffolding is in place to be transferred to other situations. One note will lead to a tune, a word or a sentence, a number to a sum, an equation to an answer – magic.

They should remember also to praise pupils at every stage. A little bit of encouragement will go a long way in the classroom. They need to ask individuals if they understand, try different approaches from lesson to lesson and keep the level of enthusiasm high.

In this introductory column, I would like to begin with a request: I do not want to feel alone in this venture. Writing and teaching can be lonely endeavours. I hope that in writing I can call on the expertise of my colleagues at Canterbury Christ Church University College and the many friends I have working in schools across the UK.

I hope, too, that I will be able to call on the community of learners who read and contribute to this column – if only to reassure myself and others in the profession that we still have time to think about learning and teaching, albeit for an hour on a Sunday evening, having marked the last set of books and prepared the lesson plans for the next week.

Questions for discussion

Having read this column, consider your place as a learner. It places Joe at the centre but what encouraged him to learn and how did others react to him in the process? A sense of place was the factor that contributed most to how and what Joe learnt, so how do you engage with learning and teaching? Consider:

1. How can the Joes of this world be identified?
2. How would you respond to Joe's needs?
3. Can you discuss Joe's needs with other practitioners?
4. How can you place learning at the centre of your practice?
5. What enables you to engage with others to encourage and stimulate learning?

What makes a good learning environment?

The holidays are here! Students and teachers feel the same, tired but rewarded by all that has been achieved. The aim for many will be to go places, to go on adventures in new and familiar places.

At this time of the year, those responsible for the timetable in schools, colleges and universities have the unenviable task of placing teachers and learners in suitable spaces. Disciplines such as physical education, art, design and technology, science, music and ICT [information and communications technology] require specialist rooms. Maths, English and humanities teachers also need artefacts and materials to assist learning.

The 'timetabler' often loses much of the summer break putting together the jigsaw of placing learners in a room with a teacher. It is often at this stage that senior managers are faced with difficult decisions.

But positively the world of education has a new professional friend – architects are now turning their attention to the design of appropriate learning spaces. Projects in Italy, Scandinavia and the US have led the way in school and college design. In the US, urban streets are closed to traffic to facilitate physical education lessons, while in Italy much is being developed in early learning to provide spaces for babies, toddlers and young learners to achieve their full potential.

Here in the UK we have seen new designs emerge, funded by private finance initiatives (PFI), local education authorities and, in the case of the new academies, philanthropists of a bygone age. The buildings that are being created are creative and sometimes feats of architectural genius. However, questions do need to be asked. Do these buildings offer the most appropriate places and spaces for learning in the twenty-first century?

Recently I had the pleasure of working with a head teacher who had been drafted in to save what had been a failing school. At the time, the school was three years old and the local authority-owned building it inhabited was two years old, funded through a PFI [private finance intiative]. In the two years of its life, the building had been vandalised by students: the graffiti on the walls was extensive; sockets and switches were broken; doors, walls and panels kicked. Yet in the entrance, there was an immaculate £5,000 pound model of the building, proudly displayed by the outgoing head teacher.

What had gone wrong? Teachers had not been consulted: the design of the building had been planned by the head teacher with the governors and other agents. The outcome? Classrooms were too small, corridors were of an open gallery style and stairwells looked and smelt like public conveniences. The one exception was the open area designed by the special educational needs coordinator (SENCO), which lacked the vandalism evident in other areas of the school.

Teachers, architects and the funders should talk. Given the large amount of funding currently being allocated for building, educators should be invited to contribute. After all, once each of the new buildings has been constructed, it will be teachers and learners who will determine where and when they use the spaces and what they will do when they get there.

Questions for discussion

Where and how learners learn is a current topic in education with discussions focusing on the style of learning as determined by the buildings in which learning takes place. The environment is no less important. Consider:

1. How does your environment impact on learning and teaching?
2. How can you improve the environment in which you teach/ learn?
3. Could your school or college enhance learning through the environment?
4. Are there plans to develop your environment? Could you contribute?

Summary

Engagement with the world we inhabit provides the framework in which we learn. The impact on the classroom of technical, social and political developments has shaped an environment which is now global and inclusive (DfES, 2004e). In response, effective teachers and learners place the child and other learners at the centre of their practice – as we live together, we learn together (DfES, 2004b).

2 Issues in education

Introduction

There are many issues which impact the practice of teaching and learning. Planners, politicians, educators and teachers are renowned for their ability to create policies 'on the hoof'. They are also known for a lack of 'joined-up thinking': that is the essence of the tale of the two crisp policies below – the importance of one practice or policy relating to another.

It is paradoxical that education policies are not 'joined up' when inclusion dominates our thinking and practice (DfES, 2004f). Inclusion is an ideology which has contributed to the raft of policies which, to some, appear to miss the point. Perhaps a more straightforward approach is needed. If learning is to be at the heart of education, 'to be included' is at the heart of inclusion.

A sense of being includes relating to a sense of community. Effective schools and colleges are integral to the community. They are a community within a community, embracing all aspects of community life (Gibson and Blandford, 2005). In the context of the 'Futures' agenda, this is likely to expand beyond the current practice as health and welfare centres are located within schools and colleges. For multi-agency practitioners, inclusion may take on yet another meaning – that of being included in professional teams.

Focusing on the individual within the community is an issue that teachers have to consider across all phases of education. Each column illustrates that the relationship between learning and teaching is complex embracing many issues. If teachers and practitioners are to understand the relationship, they will need time to reflect and space to plan.

A palatable alternative to selling crisps in school tuck shops

The status of the crisp in a young person's diet has been prominent recently in the educational and general press. The number of children who are obese has increased and poor behaviour is often attributed to diet. The variety of crisps has reached new heights. Most of us know that eating crisps is unhealthy, and yet we continue to be drawn by the richness of the market. Crisps play a part in the daily eating rituals of our pupils and students and teachers. Yet there are conflicting messages coming out from schools.

Consider the position of a parent with a child in a high school that encourages the eating of crisps and a younger child in a primary school where crisps are now banned. This is the tale of two crisp policies.

The first crisp policy is located in a local high school known to me that is currently generating funds by way of a tuck shop. The enthusiastic administrator works in partnership with the head teacher ordering the variety of goodies available for the ever hungry 11- to 16-year-olds, who contribute £1,000 pounds a month to the unofficial school fund. Crisps and other such salty snacks are in great demand, the local wholesale company is delighted with the school and the pupils spend less time off-site during lesson breaks. A further consequence of the tuck shop is that the school site is a wash of colour with empty crisp packets and sweet papers covering the ground. The site manager and staff are in revolt. But the shop is making money to subsidise the purchase of computers.

The background to the second crisp policy is rooted in an anti-crisp outburst in the infant department of a small primary school. The outburst was in response to the poor eating habits of the 5- to 7-year-olds that often resulted in a layer of crumbs on the desks, tables and floor. Class teachers had reached the end of their tether and had advised the head teacher that crisps were no longer to be eaten their classrooms. In response, the head teacher created a new anti-crisp policy followed by a letter to all parents and guardians requesting that the food pupils eat at break times should be of the fruit and fibre kind. Crisps are no longer acceptable. The school now looks forward to being a crisp-free zone, classrooms and the playground will no longer be adorned with such litter. In its place will be rotten fruit and there also might be a storage problem between breaks.

The parents of the two children now face a dilemma. One child will need the additional £1 a day to supplement the school coffers while the other will need a bag of groceries each week. The children have also discussed the matter and the younger sibling is now completely against the idea of eating an apple instead of a crisp. The answer could be that they both eat an apple, but the management of children and their rights is not quite that simple. This is set to cause discontentment and sibling rivalry each school morning.

Alternatively, the local authority could preside over a joined-up initiative to encourage all pupils and students to eat a healthy snack that could be purchased on the school site so as to raise funds as needed.

Questions for discussion

Professional practice is governed by legislation that generates policies. The relevance of policies to practice is reflected in the appropriateness of the resultant procedures. Consider:

1. Are you informed of the policies that impact on your practice?
2. What is your part in the creation of policies?
3. How inclusive is your learning community?
4. How does your professional practice relate to inclusive policies?

Inclusion is about identifying and removing injustices

The notion of inclusion in mainstream settings may have had an unfortunate beginning. Since the Warnock Report was published in 1978, which identified the needs of pupils who had restricted access to education in mainstream settings as 'special', educators have responded to the political and social drive towards inclusion.

As a consequence, social inclusion has been dictated by

policy imperatives. The more included a child is, the less need policy-makers will consider there to be for additional support.

'Effectiveness' is being gauged by a reduction in numbers of those learners who are deemed in need of 'special' education. I would tend to disagree with this line of policy-making and look towards the approach adopted by Paulo Freire, the Brazilian educationalist. 'Inclusion', he said, 'is about listening to unfamiliar voices, being open, empowering all members and celebrating differences in dignified ways. From this perspective, the goal is not to leave anyone out of school. Inclusive experience is about learning to live with one another […] it is about how, where and why, and with what consequences we educate all pupils […] and involves a serious commitment to the task of identifying, challenging and contributing to the removal of injustices.'

Margaret was 5 years old, her legs in calipers, when I first met her. She had been mentally and physically disabled from birth. She had been abandoned by her family and institutionalised, and eventually placed in the care of the Children's Society. In my early years of teaching, young musicians and I gave Christmas concerts to her 'family' in the 'home'.

After three such visits, it became apparent that she had a particular interest in music. One of the band members invited her to join.

Several weeks later Margaret, full of enthusiasm, joined the percussion section. During the following ten years, she participated in concerts at home and abroad. Her hands developed, as did her legs, so that by the age of 18 she had shed the calipers and developed social skills to enable her to find employment. Unfortunately, she was then moved to a different part of the country.

More recently I met Joseph, who was born with a severe hearing impairment. Through attending his brother's music lessons he was provided with the opportunity to pick up a euphonium. Within weeks he was able to play a tune and months later joined the beginners' windband. His lack of hearing was not a problem; he could follow the beat and be guided by his neighbour. Later Joseph passed an audition and registered as a junior exhibitionist at a college of music. All went well until he was asked to sit at the back of a large orchestra; inevitably he struggled resulting in him having to leave. He now studies art.

Given the natural capacity of young people to be critical, neither Margaret nor Joseph experienced any educational or social difficulties while working with the musicians of their own age. It was the system that eventually let them down, Joseph having been moved in the orchestra and Margaret being moved to a different area. Injustice? Possibly not, but they were not heard beyond the music.

Questions for discussion

The ideology of inclusion is dominant in all areas of society. The notion of 'to be included' regardless of socio-economic, medical, ethnic, cultural or educational background underpins educational practice, or does it? Consider:

1. What is the policy for inclusion in your school or college?
2. Is your school or college 'comprehensive'?
3. What practices are inclusive?
4. Do you have positive examples of inclusion in your school or college? Are these shared?

Time to give SENCOs the support they deserve

OfSTED has added to the proliferation of documents that focus on providing guidance and advice with the publication of a report *Special Educational Needs (SEN) and Disability: Towards Inclusive Schools* (OfSTED, 2004a). Its main findings suggest that there has been little improvement, in practice, of providing for children with SEN and few schools even evaluate their practice. Not a very positive position to be in, ten years after the introduction of a Code of Practice for SEN (DfE, 1994).

Since 1870, children diagnosed with SEN, whether social or medical, have been integrated into compulsory primary and secondary education provision. While policy-makers and educationalists have continued to stress the importance of educating all children of school age, teachers remain concerned by the management and level of resourcing associated with SEN. As it is the job of the special educational needs coordinator (SENCO) to manage staff, pupils, parents and external agents in providing the most appropriate education for these pupils, it is the SENCOs who encounter the daily concerns voiced by their colleagues.

SENCO positions are often taken by competent teachers who have a good rapport with a wide range of the school community. They are rarely trained, either as experts in SEN or as managers. Yet they take on responsibility for the most difficult and complex of tasks – the management of individual needs, each profound enough to attract additional support and funding.

More often than not, the SENCO is a middle manager who has limited status and yet is in a role deemed to be important. Most SENCOs spend a large proportion of their time teaching either additional needs classes or National Curriculum subjects or both. They are also expected to attend meetings with external agents, coordinate learning support assistants and convene meetings with pastoral and academic teams within their school. When not managing their teaching or that of others, they have a mountain of documents to prepare from the SEN/inclusion policy to individual action plans for each child with SEN.

Then there is the proliferation of papers and legislation that fall on the head teacher's desk and are passed to the SENCO. Policy-makers fail to understand that each time such a document is produced it adds to the burden of the SENCO, who has the responsibility to deliver the aims those documents set out. This will mean clarifying the needs of the workforce, agreeing staff development needs, and processing meetings required for decision-making and implementation. This is a huge task for any member of a senior leadership team, an almost impossible task for a middle manager.

Beyond management and resources SENCOs are asked by OfSTED to demonstrate their school's commitment and support of children with SEN and disability. OfSTED have the task of evaluating how children with SEN have their needs met as soon as they become apparent and often leaves SENCOs feeling extremely vulnerable.

Teacher, planner, curriculum- and people-manager, fund agent, monitor and reviewer – these are just a few of the daily roles encountered by the SENCO. Isn't it about time that they are properly trained and supported?

Couldn't all teachers in all schools be given adequate training to manage and deliver a curriculum that responded to the needs of all pupils? Would it not be appropriate for advanced skills teachers to receive training to manage individual educational plans for children with social and medical needs? Could head teachers lead policy changes? If teachers, specialists and leaders were able to support the SENCO, wouldn't this help schools to meet the inclusive aims that have featured in government policies for 135 years?

If SENCOs continue to be so overburdened, another generation of children with SEN will fail to be educated. The building of capacity to support SEN provision has to be the next priority of government, not the continuing stream of unattainable advice that continues to emanate from government agencies.

Questions for discussion

Inclusion is often deemed to be the responsibility of the SEN coordinator. Should this be so? Consider:

1. What is the SEN policy in your school or college?
2. How does this resonate with the policy for inclusion?
3. How is SEN practice supported?
4. What professional development is available for staff who engage with SEN?

Schools are a microcosm of their local community

When visiting the Cotswold village of Bourton on the Water, it is hard to resist viewing the model of the village, which itself contains a model of the village. 'The village within the village' is an image of how a school relates to its local community.

Most schools extend practice beyond the classroom into the community – a school becomes a community within a community. In addition, members of the school community will also be members of their local community: as such, they will reflect the beliefs and values of that community. These will be conveyed through the behaviour and attitudes of the school community.

The principles on which community provision is built are based on certain assumptions: education is part of social provision, strongly related to all other branches of social provision. Education does not exist as an academic entity in its own social vacuum: social provision is determined by the social and economic framework of society.

Historically, social and educational provision have become more centrally controlled, while at the local level there has been a move towards the provision of activities led by the community, with a greater emphasis on participation.

If we accept that schools are communities with local needs, pupils, teachers, parents, governors and support agencies need to relate to each other, and share an understanding of the goals and targets of an effective school. The more isolated teachers feel, the harder it will be for them to function. The organisational structure of the school would benefit by reflecting the psychological and sociological make-up of its community.

A comprehensive community plan may not be a cure-all for problems in the classroom, corridor and playground, or beyond the school gates, but in the process of identifying the needs of the school as a community, teachers, support agencies and managers can create a community ethos appropriate to their school.

A school is more than a building. All members of the school will need to take responsibility for the environment and the people that make up the community. This includes the building and its use, and a management structure that accommodates all staff and key stakeholders.

By identifying the needs of the school, all members of the school community can develop a structure that suits their school. For example, parents will need to know the system that enables them to discuss their child's education with the appropriate professional – a teacher, health visitor, social worker or educational welfare officer. Parents also need to understand the boundaries between the acceptable and unacceptable.

Clear communication will lead to clearer understanding and shared values. An emphasis on community will reflect a caring, sharing ideology, which will provide each school with a framework that focuses on people, not structures. Such practices will lead to improved home–school relations and broader usage of the school for the whole community. The village within the village will become the community within the community.

Questions for discussion

As a member of the community in which you work, consider:

1. Are you familiar with the needs and aspirations of the local community?
2. Is learning central to the community?
3. How can you impact on the social and economic growth of the community?
4. Do individuals have a place within the community of learners?

Good practice is what makes teaching a job worth having

Most readers will remember the film *The Good, The Bad and The Ugly*, the storyline being that the bad and the good are indistinguishable. Similarly, teaching is a profession that can be seen as a good or bad career choice.

Fundamentally, teachers need to feel good about their practice. There is a tendency to criticise practice and so belittle the status of practitioners.

Good practice is not an imaginary phenomenon. It happens in the majority of schools on a daily basis. Teachers should feel confident that they are able to provide a secure environment in which students learn and succeed. However, behaviour needs careful management. It is difficult to believe any senior manager who feels that a behaviour management plan is not needed for their school.

The following vignette is based on the development of good practice in a small inner-city secondary school in the West of England. The majority of pupils are from the local community, a socially disadvantaged area; many are sent to the school as a last resort, having failed at more academically successful schools. After five years of struggle with poor behaviour and examination results, the deputy head teacher, supported by the local education authority and governors, developed and implemented a behaviour management plan for the school.

The school had previously relied on school managers to address behaviour issues. Discipline was system-based, set within management structures, rather than a philosophy that was shared by all. When such structures exist, they can be leant on by those teachers who have a tendency to believe they are not responsible for the behaviour of the pupils.

Inevitably, the system was allowed to decay and teachers felt disempowered. Further training and development were required to create a policy based on shared expectations.

The low esteem in the community compounded the problem – pupils needed to be made aware that they could succeed. Expectations of pupil behaviour and work levels by staff and pupils required clearer, defined boundaries. Staff were keen to contribute. There was an emerging belief that the majority of pupils wanted an environment where they could learn.

A Code for Success became the blueprint for behaviour management, shaped by three strands of activity: clear guidelines to pupils, parents, governors and staff; agreed parental contracts and meetings and staff discussions; and finally, much needed support for staff, with directed support for difficult pupils.

An outcome of the Code for Success has been a significant improvement in pupil–teacher relationships. The school developed a very full schedule of extra-curricular activities, which built on the community's strengths. Pupil behaviour during these activities was generally good – they wanted to do well and it was possible for them to succeed. This positive behaviour has been transferred to the classroom and school corridors.

Teachers are now in a position to try new approaches including a review of teaching and learning styles, the introduction of accelerated learning programmes and the development of pupil self-confidence.

Questions for discussion

Celebrating success is a feature of organisational life. Its impact on behaviour can be evidenced by individual, team and organisational commitment to tasks, objectives, targets and each other. The age-old adage 'nothing breeds success like success' prevails – just look around. Consider:

1. How do you identify individual, team and organisational success?
2. How is this celebrated?
3. Do successes inform practice?
4. Do successes impact on visions and plans for the future?
5. Does one success lead to another?

Importance of planning

Planning is essential, a central tenet of teachers' professional practice. That came out strongly at the recent workshops for Teaching Award winners, and I remember Estelle Morris reported that the section of the Education Department's standards website on how to improve lessons once received 21,897 hits on Christmas Day.

Was it really the case that many of the nation's teachers were to deliver a government-prescribed lesson in the first week of January this year? Or was the rush of enthusiasm for curriculum planning linked to a desire to creatively interpret what is offered as a guide?

The purpose of planning is self-evident: to provide the teacher and learner with a clear, logical means of engaging with the substance of the lesson. Planning has its own structure that relates to learning, setting goals and reaching achievable outcomes. An unintended outcome of plans, however, is that they can provide the teacher with a structure that allows for deviation and creativity in the classroom. Plans allow for imagination, growth and individual learning. They provide the teacher and learner with security and the comfort of knowing what comes next, while allowing for the element of surprise that is often experienced in the classroom.

Beginning with objectives, teachers should ask of themselves: what am I trying to achieve? What are the courses of action available? Which one will best achieve my objectives? Once the actions have been identified, these can be sequenced. What resources are required? Do the objectives and/or actions need to be amended in the context of limited resources? The planner can then review the plan and times set, what to do and when.

The following analogy might be useful. We all listen to music. Whether the music is light, serious, individual or shared, most musicians are actively engaged in the creation and interpretation of plans.

A musical score is a plan followed by a performance leading to review and possible changes according to interpretation, context and resources. Within a score, a composer will set out objectives: length and style, the motifs and dynamics. Actions are encapsulated within the structure, not dissimilar to a scheme of work. Each section has its own rhythms, melodies and harmonies according to the mood and understanding the composer wishes to create. Depending on the genre of the work, the plan will be extremely detailed or provide more of a guide to performers. I know many teachers who enjoy jazz, and there are those who prefer classical or folk music. Perhaps this could account for variations in planning.

What happens when a plan comes together? When actions achieve the aims, teachers and pupils reflect on what has been learnt and link to the next scheme or lesson. When a plan becomes a performance that engages with feelings and understanding, learning will take place.

A plan can also help teacher stress levels. Entering a room where there is a shared understanding of aims and actions can be compared to listening to a performance of a favourite piece of music. Whether the focus is on entertainment, excitement, relaxation or surprise, the learning experience is more often than not a positive one. Take a look at your planning and enjoy the process.

Questions for discussion

Policies without plans will not lead anywhere. Consider:

1. How often do strategic or operational plans reflect policies?
2. How detailed are your lesson/learning plans?
3. How innovative are your plans?
4. Do you work in harmony with your neighbours – within your place of work or beyond?

Noise control – a level of distraction

Learning requires concentration which for some can only happen where the air is still and there are no distractions. There are those educators who believe that visual and aural distractions are to be avoided if learning is to take place while others rely on significant amounts of visual and aural stimuli to engage their pupils.

Early in my career I became aware just how irritating my creative and performance-orientated music lessons and after-school activities were to my colleagues. This was evidenced by two fairly dramatic events. The first was when the wind orchestra, which had grown in number rather than ability over a two-year period, was confronted by a seething deputy head. Unfortunately her office was opposite the small school hall where rehearsals took place every Monday and Friday after school.

We were rehearsing the theme tune from *Hawaii-Five-0* which had quite a repetitive rhythm: dum-de-dum, dum-de-dum, dum-de-dum and so on. After a sixth attempt of correcting the dum-diddy-dum to dum-de-dum she emerged. Apparently we had no consideration for others and should be banished to the corner of what was then quite a large school field. Evidently we could not coexist. Our use of the space was interference beyond the level of distraction.

The solution was to take our dum-de-dums to the other end of the site to the lower school hall. Here we interrupted the A-level revision sessions run by the head of mathematics, but as he was not a member of the senior management team this did not seem to matter so much.

The second event followed a move from the school hall to the local manor, using a space previously occupied by a college of art. This was in my third year of teaching; the wind orchestra had grown to over 50 players and had progressed to Sousa marches and songs from the shows. Rehearsing as we were on a Friday evening and Saturday morning, it was clearly our intention not to distract other learners.

However, the lord of the manor was still in residence and while we were in the east wing and he resided in the west, our early Saturday morning attempts at *West Side Story* were not appreciated.

As we were clearing up we met him in the entrance, where he was ready with his dogs and gun to join the local hunt. That was our last rehearsal at the house.

More recently I have been implementing room moves; the prevailing issue was that of noise. Tutors were rightly concerned that they could not share a space with someone who was constantly on the phone researching or had numerous students in their office throughout the day. This seemed perfectly reasonable.

However, there was one incident which seemed a little unusual. Intending to create space, the faculty administrator planned to move the fax machine. But this caused more consternation among staff than anticipated, because fax machines beep and for some people the beep is difficult to tolerate.

Teachers need to be sympathetic to their peers' needs, both to be quiet and to make a noise. But there are other forms of noise outside of the music, dance and drama studios. A single beep can be a distraction in itself.

Questions for discussion

Noise can be a real issue in schools and colleges. A place and space for learning may be appropriate for the individual but may also interfere with the place and space of others. Consider:

1. Do you have a policy on noise, places and spaces?
2. How do you work with others in your shared learning environment?
3. Have you discussed noise?
4. Do you have a sense of the impact of the noise generated by those in your classroom?
5. Is the noise level an indication of the effective and healthy application of policies?

Summary

Schools and colleges are accountable to the government. A measure of their success is associated with the appropriateness and impact of their policies. Yet as complex organisations, schools and colleges tend to operate vertical and horizontal strands of activity which fail to join up. Policy overload is preventing us from linking the vertical with the horizontal. The columns illustrate a common-sense approach is often all that is required to address the issues that seem to pervade our lives.

3 Leadership

Introduction

Since the implementation of the 1988 Education Reform Act, which introduced the National Curriculum, parental choice and the devolution of funding to schools, the leadership and management of schools and colleges has continued to evolve. The first phase of changes led to a headship which was dominated by the need to manage budgets and recruitment to schools and colleges. Following the introduction of the non-statutory Code of Practice for Special Educational Needs (DfES, 2001), the second phase focused on the pendulum swinging towards inclusion and the community. The next phase has seen the dominance of leadership over management in the development of schools, colleges and, more recently, higher education institutions as organisations that are market-led, collegial learning communities.

This chapter considers the role and function of leadership in education to be primarily that of leading learning, but paradoxically not one that focuses on the role of the head teacher. Leaders have power, influence and control yet they may not be the lead professional. This is the role of others in a dispersed model where competencies and attributes of the individual contribute to the extended team of leaders. The need for collaboration is self-evident. Teachers are ready to take responsibility as they develop into accountable academic leaders within their communities.

Communities require collaboration and therefore meetings. Although meetings have a bad press, not all are pointless – and are less so, as with the introduction of workforce reform teachers' contracted time is now under greater scrutiny (DfES, 2003a). The purpose of formal and informal meetings can be framed by the vision, values and principles of the school or college.

As one of the major drivers in the change to educational leadership, budgets have now been further devolved. Schools and colleges have responsibility for a significant proportion of the local and national purse; it is time for teachers with some professional development to gain experience as budget holders. After all, each teacher is well placed to become the leader of their own learning community.

Time for individual needs to take priority

As schools prepare for the next academic year, there are many adverts for leadership posts. Some make reference to the person vacating the post while others present a vision for a new future in schools through the restructuring or re-engineering of leadership teams. This gives some cause for concern when you recognise the multiple changes that have been imposed on the management of schools over the last 15 years – in practice, three generations of secondary school pupils.

Historically, the leader of a school was the head teacher, a senior colleague with expert learning and teaching skills who led by example. The emphasis was on creating a learning community. The structure was seemingly straightforward: a head, deputy and teams of teachers who taught a class or number of classes according to their subject.

Everyone appeared to know and recognise the systems that supported the structure and there were few changes.

Local management of schools and the introduction of the National Curriculum were two features of the government's grand design known as the Education Reform Act. Devolution of funding to schools was coupled with the introduction of a prescribed national curriculum. The government's aim was to raise achievement. Systems were generated to support this new structure. The position of head teachers became that of a managing director of a company, whose product is education and whose clients are pupils and parents. In the process of implementing the design, school management teams and teachers became accountable to a range of stakeholders: national and local government, governors, parents, pupils and inspectors. This was not too dissimilar to other changes within the public sector.

The response was passive and restructuring of all aspects of schooling continued apace. The government now felt the need to change the design year on year. Head teachers were trained as project managers to implement and manage budgets and in some cases become architects of new buildings. Having redesigned their schools, they now marketed their product. The head teacher became an estate agent promoting their schools in an attempt to recruit large numbers of pupils and, for additional income, the use of the building.

One outcome of this has been a growth of individual and outstanding schools. When visiting a local authority recently, I found that within a three-mile radius there were a variety of designs where unwittingly the management structure reflected the design of the building.

The emphasis had been on difference and competition but the government now wants schools to come together in the form of commonwealths, clusters, collegiates or federations. These are collective nouns for a number of schools joining together to share and develop learning communities.

What next? As tastes and needs differ I would imagine that the pendulum will swing back to individual choice. The future, I believe, will embrace the need for each learning community to respond to local and individual needs.

Questions for discussion

Leadership of schools and colleges is emerging as a priority in the majority of local authorities in England and Wales. There is significant evidence that schools and colleges are having difficulty in appointing suitable senior managers and the profession must take responsibility for the development of its own leaders. Consider:

1. What are the characteristics of an effective head teacher or principal?
2. Is it a case of 'fit for purpose' in that each school or college has its own needs?

▶

All teachers can be managers and leaders

It's behind you! Christmas, New Year have been and gone, and we are now into the pantomime season. Pantomimes were originally created by travelling players who took traditional folk tales to the stage. In many ways this is what happens in schools – the traditions of teaching are rooted in folklore substantiated by repeated practice.

Central to a pantomime are the key characters with whom audiences can identify by the end of the opening scenes. Are there parallels within school communities? Can you identify with any of the following?

● The king or duke who tries to manage his kingdom in a kind, benevolent way but is hindered by the demands of his villagers and the need to find an appropriate suitor for his single daughter.
● The dame who has been around for generations and never does what he/she is told, totally unmanageable but quite loveable.
● The village idiot, who wants to fall in love but lacks the wit and wherewithal to change and is destined to take on the role of dame in later life.
● The character that always saves the day is the principal boy (in reality a female) who, as a strong leader from humble origins (sometimes the son of the dame) identifies the problem, tackles the monsters in his/her path and manages to have a life along the way.

In the finale, there are the inevitable celebrations as the principal boy marries the princess (quite acceptable in any form). While the dame enjoys his/her newfound status as a senior member of the community the village idiot is recognised for his humility and finds a mate. The village is happy, the king can retire having led his kingdom through a period of change resulting in a positive and happy community.

Are there similar characters in your school? Given such generic characteristics, there will be schools that will feel closer than others to a pantomime. Schools as organisations find themselves being led and managed in different ways. The culture of school management is changing from a 'top-down' hierarchical model to a flatter structure, which will involve the majority of staff in the management and leadership of their school. Within the profession teachers now have to consider management to be part of their daily practice.

The process by which teachers become leaders is unclear. Training for the role is not compulsory in initial or continuing professional development until headship. In practice, all teachers are managers and leaders of the classrooms and increasingly they manage and coordinate other adults on a daily basis. A teacher is a manager of learning, managing the development of knowledge and understanding, skills and abilities of pupils.

A leader is someone who gets the job done, by knowing what he/she wants to happen, and causes it to happen by managing resources and ensuring that they are put to good use, thus promoting effectiveness. In a search for continual improvement, a leader is accountable for the performance of the unit he or she is managing, of which he or she is a part. Essentially, a leader sets a climate or tone conducive to enabling people to give of their best.

If your school is to give of its best, the key characters will need to be identified and, as in the pantomime finale, led to a point of joint and equitable celebration, perhaps?

Questions for discussion

Each character in a school or college plays his/her part in the running of the organisation. Consider:

1. Have you considered the part you play?
2. What is successful leadership?
3. Would you consider yourself to be a leader or a follower?

▶

A team doesn't pull together without effective leadership

The bells toll. The team of campanologists is practising for a new season. There are probably no more that six members, all committed to getting the sequence right. Living as I do near the normally peaceful church, I have no choice but to listen to the two-hour rehearsal held on a Thursday evening. As the bells do not stop at all in any two-hour session, I can only surmise that they are driven to perfection by a leader who is not given to reflection, discussion or team decision-making. Eventually, the limping bell ringer who has fallen a fraction of a second behind their colleagues for almost the full rehearsal clicks into place and the sequence becomes free-flowing without the 'da-dum' interruption of the previous 119 minutes. Persistence, it appears, is the key, until next week's rehearsal when the 'da-dum' returns.

The management of teams is a critical feature of effective management and leadership in schools. In the broadest sense, a team is a group of people that can effectively tackle any task that it has been set to do. Many readers will be familiar with Tuckman's stages of team development. *Forming*: at this stage the team is task-focused; followed by *storming*, as conflict arises and assumptions are challenged; successful handling at this point will enable the team to reach fresh agreement on purpose and procedures. Having negotiated the storm, a *norming* stage is reached with agreed norms and practices. All being well, the team will then be ready to perform, producing solutions rather than problems.

As a team performs, the contribution drawn from each member is of the highest possible quality, and one that could not have been called into play other than in the context of a supportive team. However, teams do not act as teams simply because they are described as such. Teamwork extends beyond the common task. In my humble view, if the bells were to stop for a few minutes, the 'da-dum' problem with appropriate support could be resolved.

In essence, a school creates its identity as a team by means of a group of people working together. Successful teams are those based on shared values and perceptions, commitment and cooperation that underpin a common purpose. To manage an effective team takes confident leadership and clear direction. The importance of reflection, discussion and decision-making cannot be overestimated.

Teachers and leaders should be in a position to recognise their place in the sequence. It is for the individual and their line manager to identify whether they are among the 'da-dummers' and in need of further support and guidance.

In the context of the daily routine, schools are all too often driven by the bells that indicate the times to move, change and refocus. Thirty-five minutes for a lesson, an hour for a meeting, rehearsals, sports and home-time. Every teacher is used to schedules and the sounds that structure the day. The sequence can appear relentless. The development of a team that allows for personal and professional growth may not be as difficult as it may seem. There comes a time when it might be opportune to stop the daily sequence of events in order to be rid of the noise. If only our campanologists would agree.

Questions for discussion

Leadership is now dispersed within schools and colleges – you are all leaders. Consider:

1. What is your leadership role within your learning community?
2. How do you relate to those who lead you?

▶

Questions for discussion continued

3. What are your professional development needs as you prepare/ function as a leader?
4. What is your leadership style?
5. Are you a self-managing networker?

No teacher is an island – they need to collaborate

Many of you will have read *All in a Day*, devised almost 20 years ago by Mitsumasa Anno. The principal theme of the book is peace, a message to be shared by the members of the global village in which we live, learn and, for some, teach.

As the authors of the book describe, children's activities are related to the very different conditions in which they live, created in part by time and climate. The book focuses on New Year's day in eight time zones, highlighting the differences in the way we look while emphasising that we are all fundamentally the same.

The main actors in the text are children of a similar age: waking, sleeping, playing, eating, interacting with the environment in which they live. The children who attend schools and colleges across the UK are also representative of a number of cultures, heritages and background, yet all have the same desire and need for food, warmth, communication and peace.

While teachers are responsible for the transmission of knowledge, this is never in isolation from the experiences learners bring to the classroom. Increasingly, schools are the only places where some children can find the peace they need to grow.

As Anno and his collaborators demonstrate, there are strong similarities and differences between children from around the globe. But teachers have similar, yet different characteristics. The similarities could include a desire to be part of a community of learners who through their practice and lives are committed to value-based education.

This is described in the European Commission report,

Learning for the 21st Century, in which the authors explain learning is a composite of learning to know, learning to do, learning to live together and learning to be. Applying this to practice would extend the role of the teacher, for in addition to the transmission of knowledge that prepares the learner for a job, there is also a responsibility for preparing them to become citizens.

Social commentators inform us that there is a social and economic need for people to be lifelong learners. Nowadays, irrespective of location, people rarely find a job for life; there is a need for lifelong learning. In theory, there has never been a better time to be a teacher.

Within the cycle of learning teachers are also lifelong learners with a need to develop further their skills. Teachers need support in maintaining and improving the achievements of the learner; fundamentally they require a basic set of tools that encompasses working with knowledge regardless of subject or discipline.

The tools will also include the training and education required to develop an ability to collaborate and work with an increasingly diverse range of professionals and learners. Returning to the simple yet powerful message of Anno's book, teachers also require the tools to develop the voice of the learner, be that adult or child.

Anno concludes the introduction by commenting that each country has a neighbourhood in which children live, beyond which there is another country that shares the same sun and moon. In this text, no child is isolated from the others. The same could be said of learners and teachers.

Questions for discussion

Education does not happen in isolation. There is an interaction with knowledge which is created, generated and delivered within a social context. Our knowledge of the world is increasing as is our ability to communicate and collaborate within a global setting (DfES, 2004e). Yet collaboration remains a difficult concept for those who fail to grasp the fundamentals of networking. Consider:

▶

Questions for discussion continued

1. How wide is your professional network?
2. Have you a sense of the learner's place when you teach?
3. Do you collaborate with others?
4. How do your collaborative networks impact on your learning and teaching?
5. Do you use your knowledge to develop an understanding of the world for yourself and others?

Meetings are not a waste of teachers' time

The first meeting I chaired as a head of faculty in a secondary school will remain forever in my memory. I had set an agenda that I considered to be full, challenging and with a sense of purpose. That was the theory. In practice, the response from colleagues was muted almost to the point of a silent revolution.

I had failed to consult them on what was their meeting: papers had not been circulated; and there was little preparation and a great pile of material that could have been circulated in other ways. I had failed to respect my colleagues as members of a learning community.

It has to be said that attending meetings is not always a productive use of a teacher's time. It is useful to consider before planning a meeting whether it is necessary. This is not to say that there are not many advantages to holding a meeting: increased communication, the opportunity to improve staff decision-making skills while creating a sense of involvement and ownership. The quality of decision-making and communication are dependent on the quality of the meeting. A good meeting, if democratic, can improve job satisfaction.

The size and culture of the school will determine the number, culture and style of meetings and determine their effectiveness. If the quality of school meetings is to improve, it is necessary for all staff to understand the function of each meeting. Chairs are required to plan, lead and participate in meetings, to influence (and understand) policy, to monitor and evaluate, to solve problems and plan, to develop cooperation and commitment and, most importantly, to motivate.

There are usually two key roles in formal meetings: chair and secretary (minute-taker). It may be that teachers will be required to chair team meetings and to act as secretary to senior management or staff meetings. It is not advisable to chair and take minutes simultaneously. The collective functions of the chair and secretary are to move the meeting along efficiently and to maintain the meeting as a viable working group.

As I learnt from my initial experience of chairing, if a meeting is to be worthwhile, an agenda could be prepared in advance to allow members to consider each point and allow other points to be added to the agenda. And remember, distribute the necessary papers. Open the meeting and state its purpose, then take those present through the agenda, leaving time for reflection and discussion. Listen and value all participants in the meeting and close with a summary of the way forward and thanks.

There are a few guiding rules that will assist with the meeting's progress: ensure fair play, and stay in charge by controlling the length and depth of discussions. Take decisions in the appropriate manner – conduct a vote or check consensus, as this will encourage participation. All being well, there will be some actions that will need to be pursued and outcomes can be presented again at future meetings.

As with teaching, effective chairing requires good interpersonal skills – participants need to feel valued. A meeting will be a learning experience when the alternative uses of the participants' time are forgotten from the outset.

Questions for discussion

When we meet with others in a professional setting, there is a clear sense of purpose: to network, to engage with professionals and to learn from the experience. The knowledge and experience generated by the collective experience of the team will inform the practice, which underpins the delivery of the curriculum in schools and colleges. Consider:

▶

Questions for discussion continued

1. What is the purpose of each meeting you attend?
2. Is your role within each meeting passive or active?
3. How do you disseminate the knowledge gained from a meeting?
4. Do you follow up on the information generated at each meeting?
5. How do you ensure that meetings contribute to the function of education, i.e. the discovery and exchange of information and knowledge?

Teachers should seize the chance to become budget holders

When preparing a budget for a bid, extra-curricular activity or an increase in curriculum funding, many teachers are left floundering. This is due not to a lack of ability so much as a lack of experience, a consequence of limited opportunities created by a particular style of leadership and administration.

Limited opportunities could arise from concerns over external accountability, which tends to drive the management of school finances. Budget management is not contingent on schools alone – the actions of central and local government set the framework and content of a school's funding arrangements.

Within a framework of collaborative management, teachers would have an opportunity to develop professionally through involvement in financial management. They could become a budget holder with responsibility for a sum of money to be spent on a particular subject, year group or other specific purpose.

As my colleague Simon Hughes suggests (Hughes, 2004) in his book *Subject Leaders: Resource Management*, successful budget management is facilitated by the individual skills and attributes of each person. Such individual skills will thrive in a context that has effective and efficient managerial systems.

I believe that success in financial management requires a shared sense of responsibility on the part of the staff in the school to enhance both the pupil performance and the physical environment. Once these principles and values have been determined, the capacity for growth can be informed by organisational intelligence that will assist planning for the future.

A useful starting point for a budget holder is to compare financial statements from the previous years within similar departments and teams. This will help to identify areas where money could be saved and those that need funding, beginning with basic needs and concluding with additional operational expenditure.

Linked to the school development plan, this budget planning would involve identifying priorities and targets. It is usually advisable to aim to spend all of the allocated funds for teaching materials and staff. Remember, schools are places of learning, not global businesses seeking to accrue wealth. I would suggest that allocation models that identify costs set against actual needs will provide the best financial and educational returns.

Be warned: there are consequences of operating devolved budget management and accountability systems in schools. The change in the power relationship between budget holder and management might possibly lead to distrust and a tendency to resist change culminating in internal conflict.

However, the dangers of pseudo-participation – where all stakeholders are involved at the planning and decision-making stages but decisions are made by management – are far greater. Budgets that assist the drive to meet agreed educational targets will be more successful than those designed to lead. My advice to teachers is to become a budget holder, then understand and contribute to the principles and values that underpin your school's financial management.

Questions for discussion

Financial management in schools and colleges is often misunderstood (Blandford and Blackburn, 2004). Myths can be generated by those who feel uninformed and marginalised by practices that are owned by the few but impact on the many. Professional practice is about taking charge, including financial matters. Consider:

▶

Questions for discussion continued

1. How transparent are the financial management systems within your school or college?
2. Do you have sufficient information on the availability of resources prior to developing the curriculum?
3. Are you responsible for the management of budgets allocated to your area?
4. What professional development opportunities are available to enhance your budget management?
5. Do you engage with budget management in a collaborative environment?

Summary

In educational organisations, leadership is a complex phenomenon. There are many definitions of leadership which share the common themes of power, culture and influence. It is evident that leadership happens in groups or teams, a social context that embraces organisations including schools and colleges. As in teaching, leaders direct a group in order to achieve something together. With leadership there is fellowship. A further dimension to consider is the global context in which we live. This creates an additional responsibility for teachers who might be viewed as cultural negotiators and workers. Whatever the context, education leadership begins within our own setting – the classroom. How we interact with others will be informed by a range of factors that are influenced by the individual and collaborative contexts in which we work.

The economic status of the organisation is rarely understood in education, yet it is a significant factor in teaching and managing practice. In a collaborative model of leadership, an understanding of budgets will inform those responsible for practice. This would also facilitate an understanding of the relationship between professional values and financial management (Blandford and Blackburn, 2004). Leadership is a domain that has its own repertoire, theories and practice that encourage the self-managing networker.

4 Classroom practice

Introduction

This chapter is essentially concerned with what takes place within a place of learning, the classroom, whether this place be a space with tables, whiteboard and displays, lecture theatre or one located beyond the school or college building.

To capture an understanding of how learning takes place is not possible within a few columns; however, a raising of awareness might be achievable. As the government has indicated (DfES, 2004b), personal safety and security are essential prerequisites to learning. Creative stimuli can also help, but this is not all. Learners of all ages also feel secure when there is a sense of progression, a sense of 'where next'?

Personal safety and a sense of direction can be threatened by the behaviour of others. Teachers, parents, learners, OfSTED and educators are in agreement that behaviour in schools has deteriorated. Many children engage in low-level behaviour that impacts negatively on the learning environment. Unfortunately and often, teachers can be innocent contributors to such behaviour. At one end of the continuum they may spend part of their day shouting; at another end they may fail to know when to identify and seek professional help for the learner and themselves.

Many schools have tackled the issue of behaviour in a positive way whereby behaviour for learning is commonplace (Powell and Tod, 2004). Learning is informed by assessment; in the majority of cases, teachers are proficient at feeding back to both children and, when appropriate, parents or guardians. Given the complexities of the assessment regime and subsequent examination system this is nothing short of a miracle.

As a visit to the classroom would demonstrate, there is much to celebrate in schools and colleges. Teachers and practitioners can reflect on, and enjoy, the positives. However, professionals should not be complacent; classroom practice requires fresh, innovative thinking. Time out is therefore critical if teachers are to be effective professionals. Here Nemo's friends give good advice on how to relax and consider our place in the world.

Pupils thrive in structured, creative mess

Location, location, location – so we are told when buying a home. It's a pity that we do not have the same freedom in where we teach. When working in London I began each morning by joining the caretaker in chasing rats out of the performing arts block. The block, named after Dame Peggy Ashcroft, was situated between the Thames and the Grand Union canal, with broken sewers under the footings. Once gone, the rats left us alone until the close of play at the end of the day. My reason for chasing them was simple: my pupils and I enjoyed working in a safe, clean and healthy environment.

The aim of the school was to create a good sense of belonging and order that created a healthy, supportive environment for learning. As a teacher, I was responsible for ensuring that the classroom was tidy and ready for lessons at the start of day. In achieving this aim I found it useful to have a good relationship with the caretaker and cleaners – the keepers of the keys are important.

Maintaining a classroom can be a challenge, particularly if the space is shared. Agreement on how chairs, tables and other equipment should be stacked and placed is a help. This will enable lessons to begin in an ordered fashion. In all learning contexts – classrooms, fields, laboratories or computer rooms – bags and coats need to be out of the way. As adults we would complain if we did not have a place for our belongings close to where we work and all members of our school communities deserve the same respect.

Much of classroom management is common sense – a messy and disorganised teaching area will lead to messy and disorganised learning. Equally, pupils will thrive in structured, creative mess … your need to strike a balance. Even in the best and worst of buildings, floors and walls can be improved. In the school with the rats, I was able to carpet the Ashcroft block with off-cuts from the new BSkyB offices. They even supplied the carpet fitter! Good use of display areas might go part way to covering up poor decoration and brightening a room. Students from Key Stage 1–4 enjoy seeing their work displayed – all of them not just the neatest or the best. Members of each class can be responsible for an area, which helps to create a sense of ownership that develops respect for the environment.

Classrooms are located along corridors, where the maintenance of floors and walls should also be of the highest order. There are 101 ways to restrict the amount of movement around a school, but at some point at the opening or close of play the management of large numbers will be inevitable. Other than training for the rugby world cup there is not much to be gained by setting one group against another – one-way systems have been seen to work in small, medium and large schools.

My final comment concerns a basic necessity – loos. Why do we allow school loos to be smelly and covered in graffiti? Not far from where I live there is a public convenience that has been awarded Loo of the Year, 2003. The rooms are clean, with tiles that sparkle, the toilets flush and the washing area is in good working order. Think of the impact on the students if they were able to use a facility that was safe, vandal-proof and had a pleasant odour. A project for the school council perhaps?

Questions for discussion

Where we learn will often determine how we learn; hi-tech settings or open fields are quite different yet both can be places that provide the learner with the stimulus to engage and develop. There is a range of experts whose perspectives on learning and the learner will help inform our practice; neuroscientists and architects are examples of those with whom a relationship could further enlighten our thinking. Teachers may learn from such expertise but it is the impact on practice that will demonstrate the true value of each perspective. How do practitioners create an environment that encourages cultural, social and intellectual development? Consider:

1. Does your school or college provide a safe and stimulating environment for its learners?
2. Have you discussed how to develop the environment with colleagues and other experts?
3. How does the place and space in which you teach impact on your style of teaching and learning?
4. What next? Will you engage with the architects and others in determining the future?

Learning should be staged like scaffolding with the next level visible

Henry, 8, loves maths. Yet his teachers find him a challenge; he talks, shouts and has been known to be involved in the occasional fight. At home, Henry's mother finds herself, in her late twenties, a single mum with two children, earning a living as a foster mother to others. Henry loves his mother and treats her with considerable respect but thinks that she is useless at maths. Henry is the man in his family.

Henry would dearly love to be stimulated. He finds his lessons boring and has often completed all tasks way ahead of his classmates. While the presentation of his work leaves a lot to be desired, the content is usually correct. Such is his frustration with the classroom, he is often removed and is to be found wandering the corridors.

Henry's mother feels that at secondary school she was ignored, so education passed her by. She knows that she is able, articulate and has a good imagination. Her use of language and awareness of the needs of children extends far beyond her current situation and background. She would like to be in a situation where she could make choices, for herself and her children.

Henry's mother recently visited her local further education college to inquire whether she would be in a position to embark on a course leading to teaching. She was told that there were no opportunities, and if there were, she was underqualified and would therefore not be accepted onto a programme. Disappointed, she resigned herself to a further ten years of fostering children and, in consultation with social workers, planned the next stage to become a carer.

A more supportive response from the college would have been to direct her to the local HE [higher education] institution, which runs foundation degrees in early years related disciplines. This has an access programme and on completion students can move to a two-year teaching programme. The choice is there for Henry's mother; with dedication and commitment she could become a teacher within four years.

Henry has a more challenging task. He has been labelled as someone who does not want to learn. A year ago, his school sent him to the doctor, who advised him to take up a hobby. Henry is now third in his age group in the area's judo club where he displays self-discipline beyond his years. His need to learn is self-evident – he talks fast and is curious as to how and why things and people work.

The Russian educationalist, Vygotsky (1962), described how learning should be staged like scaffolding. This is a model that would suit Henry, one where he could see the next task ahead of him, know that it would be challenging and be in a position to celebrate the outcome. Workforce reform might help – a teaching assistant or learning mentor could help the teacher to help Henry. The preparation of a ladder of learning in all subjects will help him to transfer the skills he has gained through maths to other subjects.

Seeing Henry succeed would be a satisfying outcome for all concerned. Henry's teachers should be able to help, guide, support and educate – to enable Henry to make the choices for himself. Education has to be the key that opens the door to a new future for both Henry and his mother.

Questions for discussion

The stages and ages that provide indicators of when and how we learn are no longer considered to be solely in the childhood domain. Lifelong learning has been embraced by the majority of organisations who provide opportunities for members of their community to be learners. In this rush for community learning, the importance of the individual cannot be lost. The next step for learning will be determined by individual need. Consider:

1. Do you plan for the individuals in your classroom?
2. Have you consulted with colleagues on individual educational plans for all learners?
3. How do you engage with the learning mentors in your school or college?
4. How does the learning and teaching policy assist your practice?
5. What are your professional development needs that will underpin existing and new approaches to learning and teaching?

Threats quash bad behaviour but positive reinforcement has lasting effect

A well-known head teacher in Middle England once demonstrated over a sustained period how he changed the behaviour of his pupils and staff by talking to them firmly but nicely. Behaviour that is rewarded tends to be repeated. In the classroom, this basic principle has been expressed under various names: positive feedback, reinforcement, operant conditioning, behaviour modification, assertive discipline.

Focusing on positive aspects is far more rewarding for teachers than focusing on punishments and threats. There is a contradiction between engaging pupils in the process of learning and threatening to punish them if disaffected or disruptive.

In practice, a teacher must use rewards and praise and, if necessary, punishments and warnings. To be effective, teachers need to be realistic in their expectations of the class and individuals, and place more emphasis on rewards and encouragement than on blame. Teachers must be ready to learn from colleagues and pupils, they must be receptive to new situations and ideas. Above all, a teacher must be fair and consistent.

Positive reinforcers include smiles, verbal approval, tangible rewards, earned points, commendations and the appreciation of peers and teachers. The only way a teacher knows if a reinforcer is positive is to see if it encourages productive behaviour.

The problem with negative reinforcers is that, while they may reduce the questionable behaviour, they do not necessarily create productive results. Punishment can be a double-edged sword, because of pupils' desire for attention. They may become heroes among their peers for being reprimanded in class.

There are other strategies for modifying behaviour. Teachers may focus on a specific behaviour, or aspect of behaviour, to develop a pupil's ability to improve. For example, a pupil who cannot concentrate for a whole lesson may be encouraged to focus on the introductory session. A teacher will ignore unproductive behaviour, with the aim of extinguishing it.

No policy, procedure or school rule ever altered pupils' behaviour on its own. It is the quality of the interactions with pupils in the use of rewards and other consequences that will make the biggest impact on good behaviour. To work this way effectively means considering carefully what strategies are available and, crucially, how to employ them.

A vital part of encouraging good behaviour is rewarding it when it happens. Teachers play an important role in noticing small instances of good behaviour and giving the pupil positive feedback with smiles, nods, and phrases such as 'well done'.

For behaviour that interferes with basic rights or breaks the rules, the logical response would be to get the pupil to make a better choice. Following the poacher/gamekeeper principle, pupils who take ownership of an issue learn self-control that will be sustained beyond the classroom and school. A quiet word will have a greater impact than a shout, as will a smile, thumbs-up or a symbolic reward such as a sticker or merit. Pupils are no different from adults – they like to be talked to firmly but nicely.

Questions for discussion

The reality of schools and colleges is determined by those who participate in compulsory and post-compulsory education. For many, irrespective of socio-economic factors, their place in the world is unstructured and dysfunctional. Schools and colleges can provide a safe, secure environment that will nurture the individual within a community. In this context, how to become a citizen within society is a shared responsibility of schools and colleges. Consider:

1. What are the shared values and goals of your school or college?
2. How are these values and goals communicated?
3. Are the values and goals evident in practice?
4. Does the behaviour of the majority of learners reflect the values and goals of the school or college?
5. How can the members of the community be encouraged to develop as citizens within a broader setting?

Successful teachers focus on learning not behaviour management

The media often comments on the negative aspects of teaching, and behaviour management appears to be a recurring theme. Behaviour management is an industry in its own right and schools are persuaded to spend large amounts of money for the wisdom of consultants. Yet those who succeed in teaching are those who focus on learning, not on behaviour.

Most teachers would agree that pupils should have access to the best quality education, which promotes equality of opportunity. The development of self-esteem and self-confidence are fundamental. Both are essential to an individual's ability to self-manage – in other words, to behave.

Learning requires an active commitment from pupils. In practice, pupils have a right to skilled care and treatment and to individual respect, and to be treated with dignity and fairness. For those pupils who disrupt lessons, by bullying, fighting or being generally abusive in some way, the sequence of events that follows can be both ineffective and frightening, leading to a recurrence of disruptive behaviour. Visiting a school as a researcher, I witnessed an example of what not to do.

Following a relatively low-level disruption, a pupil was sent out along the corridor to the subject coordinator to receive a verbal warning. The pupil returned to the class, to be reprimanded a second time, at which point he was isolated from his peers. In response, the pupil repeated the disruptive behaviour and was sent to the head of year, who gave what was now a second verbal warning.

During the following lesson in the same classroom with the same teacher, the pupil continued to be disruptive and was sent to the key-stage coordinator. A report was written and passed to the deputy head teacher. By the end of the school day, the pupil had been in a classroom for less than 20 minutes.

Things began to get serious when the pupil was summoned to explain his actions to the deputy head teacher. As this was the day after the incident, the pupil became frustrated with his own inability to remember what had happened and lost his temper whereupon the deputy head teacher phoned to invite his parents to a meeting to discuss their child's behaviour.

The meeting involved the pupil, class teacher, head of year, key stage coordinator and deputy head teacher. Various accounts were given while the parents sat and listened to their child being chastised. The outcome of the meeting was a recommendation to the head teacher that the pupil be excluded for the remainder of the week. Thus the pupil had had the opportunity to be present in a classroom for 40 minutes out of a possible 30 hours.

What had the pupil learnt? Possibly, that as a consequence of a relatively minor misdemeanour, he would be removed from the classroom to sit outside the deputy head teacher's office and finally be sent home. For a pupil with low self-esteem and self-confidence, the long-term effects are self-evident.

Alternatively the teacher might have held a brief conversation as the pupil walked into the second lesson, asking him to concentrate on learning, which may have produced a far more meaningful outcome.

Questions for discussion

Children and adult learners form relationships with their teachers. Trust is at the core of these relationships; the teacher and learner who trust each other can engage in learning without prejudice. When trust is replaced by control, learning suffers. The negotiation that preceded trust can happen in an instant or take several hours, weeks or months of practice. Consider:

1. As a pedagogue, is learning at the centre of your practice?
2. What is your relationship with the learners in your school or college?
3. How do you share learning with others in your community?
4. How do the 'others' share learning with you?
5. Are you confident that you engage with all learners?

The referee in the classroom – expectations and rules

As Wales were playing England in the recent rugby World Cup quarter finals, the referee asked number 22 to stand up and number 22 stood up. Three days later, in a European football match, when the referee awarded the home team a free kick following a clear foul by an away player, he was surrounded by so many players his assistants had to come to his rescue.

There are many reasons for the difference in approach and response. In rugby, the rules are clearly stated and understood by players and supporters alike; this is similarly the case in football. However, in rugby, when and if infringements occur, players and supporters know what to expect. During a football match,

screamers and dissenters are rarely punished – I have yet to see an advantage offered to the opposing side as a result of arguing with the referee.

Where boundaries are unclear and rewards and sanctions not set, the outcome is self-evident: players can argue with the person in charge. In the classroom, this is the teacher's responsibility. A culture in which pupils and teachers know and understand expectations and consequences is one where learning has a chance.

It is clear in rugby that the referee is in frequent communication with the players, instructing and directing throughout the game. This is not the case in football where the only encouraging whistle is at the start of the match. All others lead to punishment. In practice, it would appear that for players the only option is to argue.

Discipline is central to effective schools and effective classrooms. As professionals, all teachers are responsible for managing discipline in schools. Critical to practice is the relationship between teachers, pupils, parents, carers, families, senior leadership, governors, local education authority support agencies, educationalists and central government – these form the school community.

Just as in football and rugby, all members of the school community will have a shared understanding of discipline policy, procedures and practices. When effective, these will lead to self-control. Self-control is an outward manifestation of the ability of individuals to discipline themselves. This is evident by the individual's attitude and response to others and the environment.

When boundaries of acceptable behaviour are shared, this allows schools to function as harmonious and humane communities conducive to learning. Where boundaries are accepted, pupils will have the opportunity to develop the self-control required to manage their behaviour and attitudes without authority figures.

There is a second message to be learnt from the rugby World Cup: consistency. Consistency can be a problem in the behaviour of any organisation, not least in educational practice, when there are so many variables that influence teaching and learning. Again, this resonates with the players' understanding of shared boundaries and expectations. If all members of the school community were self-disciplined individuals, treated with respect in an environment that is safe and secure, there would be very few problems. How long does it take number 22 to stand up in your classroom?

Questions for discussion

A pedagogue is a highly trained practitioner, a professional who is an expert in learning and teaching. This European model for teaching extends beyond the notion of teaching as a clinical or technical profession which currently prevails in the United

Kingdom. For the pedagogue, the emphasis is on the development of the whole child rather than the transfer of knowledge. The expertise demonstrated by pedagogues has much to offer those schools and colleges who appear to practise a model that conspires against rather than inspires learners to participate in a shared understanding of education. Consider:

1. Is your practice knowledge-driven or based on an understanding of pedagogy?
2. Do you and your learners have shared expectations in understanding the importance of their development as learners?
3. How do you convey your expectations and the needs of learners to other practitioners in your classroom?
4. Are you consistent in maintaining your expectations of yourself and others?

Rewards and praise work much better than threats and punishment

Craig was 13 years old when his world changed. His parents divorced and he moved schools in order to join his mum living in a rented flat. His mum was busy creating a new life for herself. In every sense, Craig was left to look after himself. His parents ignored him, so he ignored them. There was little, if any, interaction between them. In textbook style Craig fell in with a 'bad lot', his behaviour deteriorated and his schoolwork suffered.

Craig was fortunate in that he attended a school that encouraged growth and development. It had a highly developed structure for learning that integrated the social, pastoral and academic. It functioned as a community that created a sense of belonging and encouraged growth. At the heart of the school was a system of rewards. All teachers in the community recognised that rewarding a pupil can happen in different forms: social rewards, for example a smile, thumbs-up or verbal feedback; symbolic rewards, for example a cup, certificate or sticker; special activities, for example playing a favourite game or choosing a learning activity;

token economies, e.g. collecting points towards another reward. Teachers recognised that telling Craig how to behave was only part of his development – positive reinforcement was essential.

Knowing the rewards, consequences and rules that operate in life and in a school are clearly vital for the effectiveness of all members of the community. However, no policy, procedure or school rule ever altered pupils' behaviour by itself. The quality of the interactions between Craig and his teachers would ultimately have the biggest impact on his behaviour and learning.

Behaviour that is rewarded tends to be repeated. This approach requires teachers to have a strategy that focuses on pupils' 'here-and-now' actions, with only those behaviours that can be seen and recorded objectively used in managing behaviour. Focusing on the positive aspects of professional practice is far more rewarding for teachers than focusing on punishments. There is a contradiction between engaging pupils in the process of learning and threatening to punish them.

When we reflect back on our own schooling, the effective teachers were those who were realistic in their expectations and placed a greater emphasis on rewards and encouragement than on blame and accusations. They learnt from both colleagues and pupils. In many situations, forethought, preventive action and positive interventions had avoided the need for sanctions. Above all, they were fair and consistent.

In supporting Craig his teachers felt confident that they had the support and guidance of senior leaders and external agents. Working together, the school community had addressed Craig's needs and he had taken responsibility for his behaviour. He was ready to learn.

The important elements in Craig's story were firmness, fairness and consistency. Put simply, he was recognised and valued as a member of his community. Quiet praise from his teachers at the start of each lesson and a target book with agreed expectations led to a sense of achievement. By the end of the year, he had gained sufficient attendance and behaviour points to join his group on their annual trip to Alton Towers. *Coda*: Craig's mum and dad woke up to the change in their son and attended parents evening – together.

Questions for discussion

In our multi-dimensional society, children experience complex relationships. Within this context, the only constant feature for those of compulsory school age might be the community created by their school or college. For extended or community schooling to succeed (Street, 2005), the functionality of practitioners will also extend beyond the classroom to the community. Consider:

1. Is your relationship with your learners positive? How can it be improved?
2. How do you encourage learners in your classroom? Is your approach punitive?
3. As a member of the learning community, what rewards are on offer to others and yourself?
4. Do you model good behaviour in the way you communicate with others?

Communication in schools should be in a quiet way and shouting is outlawed

Watching the recent BBC documentary focusing on the experiences of a range of teachers, school leaders and a school bus driver caused me to reflect on how adults and pupils communicate with each other during a school day. There are those teachers who take a controlled quiet approach, which seems to be appropriate even with the most difficult and recalcitrant students. Talking to other human beings in a sensitive, respectful manner seems to encourage a sensitive, respectful response.

In contrast there are a significant number of teachers, school leaders and professionals who unwittingly fall into the trap of conversing *al fortissimo* with pupils and each other. Why, it must be asked, do the shouters find themselves in the position of having to raise their voices above all others? This is neither sensitive nor respectful.

There are times, depending on the context, when shouting may be a form of communication that has positive overtones; shouting for joy is a good example of when we humans like to raise our voices in celebration. However, there are many examples of when shouting can be considered controlling, abusive or even violent.

Picture the terror in a child's face when they are subjected to shouting by a parent, teacher or another pupil. Yet there are members of the profession who speak in a raised tone from Monday morning to Friday evening. In any other profession such behaviour would be considered to be intolerable. Imagine doctors shouting at patients or lawyers screaming at the bench: such scenes would not be acceptable.

On a visit to a large comprehensive school in the south-west of England I was struck by a lack of awareness by a school leader as to how she communicated with her pupils. At 8.15 am, I was put into an office (book cupboard) ahead of a meeting. For the next 20 minutes she hurled abuse at every child entering the school, shouting orders and comments on their dress, behaviour and physical characteristics.

When the bell sounded to indicate the start of the day she retrieved me from the cupboard and took me into her office. I asked her whether she felt that every child was valued in the school. Her response was yes; she and her staff supported every child and aimed to help them achieve their highest potential.

For whatever reason she had failed to recognise her own behaviour as having a negative impact on the pupils she abused. This is not surprising when all verbal communications in the school were pitched at such a dynamic level that shouting was considered to be the norm.

In a neighbouring school, the situation could not have been more different. Staff and pupils spoke quietly to each other; they actually talked, listened and learned. This wasn't difficult – there was no magic ingredient other than an awareness that shouting was unacceptable.

Wouldn't it be good if all schools were managed in such a quiet, calm and peaceful manner? This would leave shouting for the good times, not the bad.

Questions for discussion

Our range and scope of communication is increasing. How and what we communicate is fundamental to the effectiveness of our ability to educate. Beyond the transmission of knowledge, we communicate spiritual, moral and educational values by the nature of our interactions with others. Consider:

1. How effective are you as a communicator?
2. What mechanisms do you use to communicate with others in your learning community?
3. Do you reflect on the nature of your communication with learners?
4. How do others communicate with you?
5. Do you shout when times are good or just when they are bad?

Children who have not learnt how to behave need expert help

Pupils and students are required to leave schools for a variety of reasons. For those aged 16 and under the reason is often behaviour. Jane, 14 and in year 10, has a history of short-term and permanent exclusions. Since infant school, she has been permanently excluded from no fewer than five schools. Her behaviour is of the irritating, indolent kind; she swears at teachers and constantly seeks attention by tapping her ruler or foot against the table. She is not malicious or violent, yet somehow she just doesn't fit in.

For the majority of the school population there are many reasons to behave well that are not evident to Jane. No amount of talking, punitive measures or exclusions have persuaded her that schools are the place for her. So what is to become of Jane? There is no simple solution. Behaviour is not something to be cured; it is intrinsic to all our activity, including learning.

Recently, I was watching a

father with his six-month-old daughter. He was not trying to get her to behave as such; he simply wanted to form a relationship. Using the child's chosen toy, he talked and smiled while keeping an eye on her gaze, rewarding her every effort to respond. He secured her attention by responding to her, ensuring that they shared participation and enjoyment in the activity. In time he would probably be likely to introduce his child to peers in order to encourage sharing and social interaction through play.

There is much to learn from normal development in natural settings that can be transferred to behaviour for learning. Infants learn to communicate and to develop a confidence in their abilities that enables them to function in group settings. If deprived of these experiences, people often find it difficult to learn in schools. While it is the role of the teachers to enhance learning behaviour, they cannot be responsible for developing good behavioural practices in infants.

So perhaps for the sake of the Janes of this world, teachers should focus on what they want to achieve by behaviour management, to create a classroom environment where all pupils feel safe and can learn.

There is the general assumption that if pupils could learn to behave well, they would learn more. This is generally followed by a further assumption that if pupils learnt more they would be better able to gain qualifications and employment, which may lead to a reduction in teenage pregnancies or crime. Unfortunately for Jane, her family and school may not have provided her with the opportunity to learn to behave. All is not lost, given that there are other options available – perhaps Jane's parents and teachers should look to alternative agencies able to focus on her needs.

Set within the context where government, media, schools, support agencies, pupils and their parents are all concerned with tackling behaviour in schools, would it not be possible for the good practice found in specialist behaviour units to be either transferred to the school context or placed alongside schools? Creating an environment that encourages behaviour for learning involves acknowledging diversity in our society.

Questions for discussion

Adaptability and flexibility are fundamental skills for the future employment of those we educate. A prerequisite of these skills is self-management, or behaviour for learning, which is a transferable skill learnt at home and school and applied to the workplace. As a pedagogue, you will facilitate self-management in learners. Consider:

1. How do you create an environment that encourages behaviour for learning?
2. Do your learners know how to self-manage?
3. How developed are your self-management skills?
4. Do practitioners work as a team to develop behaviour management strategies in your school or college?
5. Is there sufficient expertise within your school or college to support learners with behavioural problems?

Good teachers focus on what each pupil can do

A few years ago, when teaching GCSE music to what can only be described as a diverse group of students, I was subject to a local authority inspection focusing on differentiation. The music adviser observed my lesson on creative music, in which the content was almost entirely practical. For once the group responded as one, and their performance in creating a number of short compositions was masterful. I was proud of their grasp of the key elements of music.

But the inspector's feedback was entirely critical of an apparent lack of differentiation. Each of the pupils had tackled the task in their own way, yet the inspector had felt that this had not been a truly differentiated lesson. We talked it through. He felt that I needed to place each of the pupils within three groups: gifted, able and those with needs. He also suggested that he could help with the next lesson to demonstrate how to teach those with needs. Welcoming this, I agreed to team teach the next session. The inspector would teach those with needs and I would teach the others.

The aim of the lesson was for the group to understand intervals (the position of a note in relation to another) through melody and harmony. This would entail singing, playing and notation leading to the performance of a short madrigal. In practice, I had nine pupils and the inspector three. His specific task was to teach the two parts, soprano and alto, and for the pupils to analyse four bars. To his horror he found that one of the pupils could not read music – she related each note to the steps in the block of flats where she lived. The inspector worked with her to read the notes on the page but he could not achieve this.

At the end of the session the class sang the madrigal and were able to analyse intervals. The gifted had begun to apply the basic rules of harmony to their analysis: the others were able to count the steps and to recognise major and minor. At this point our most needy pupil demonstrated the full extent of her abilities; she sang the soprano line beautifully and was able to at least count each interval aurally. The inspector was quite amazed by the sudden transition from a pupil who could not name the notes on the page to one who was able to perform and analyse at GCSE level.

As an educator who wanted to learn from the experience, the inspector asked his pupil how she was able to perform in such a way. She told us how as the youngest of 11 children she had often been left in a corner of a room with an older brother's tape recorder. She loved the tapes of popular tunes that had been rejected by her older siblings. She felt comfortable with a range of music and had always been able to sing a tune. It was this that gave her confidence and why she could risk seeing how far she could go with her singing.

In the context of my music group the issue was not differentiation, more the need to find the most appropriate learning style for each pupil – in this case aural and visual – thus focusing on what each pupil can do rather than what they find difficult. As T.S. Eliot said, 'Only those who risk going too far can possibly find out how far you can go.'

Questions for discussion

Independent learning is now commonplace in schools and colleges. Workforce reform has enabled teachers to concentrate on
individuals with the support of a range of practitioners now
working in the classroom. Identifying the needs of learners is to
facilitate the discovery of knowledge and skills, to make sense of
events and places and to learn how to learn. Consider:

1. What practices facilitate independent learning in your classroom?
2. Does your curriculum encourage the learner to learn?
3. Do you allow your learners to be risk takers?
4. Do you allow yourself to take risks in the classroom?
5. Is your curriculum exciting, challenging, developmental and
   creative?

Assessment should be a means to improve teaching

The examination season now drawing to a close is, for teachers and students alike, a period of intense activity that aims to capture the knowledge and understanding of the learner. Yet participants experience highs and lows as the pressure of the occasion impacts on their performance on the day. This has led many in the education community to question the purpose and effectiveness of examinations as a means of assessment.

Put simply, the purpose of assessment and reporting is to provide an indication of achievement. But more importantly, it should assist students and teachers in the process of learning, while evaluating the curriculum and providing information for third parties (assessment authorities, parents, colleagues, the media and the government). When assessing an individual, it is the head teacher's responsibility to comply with government arrangements. In practice, teachers will complete a range of these including identification of arrangements for 'ach pupil, ensuring that the school's standards conform to national requirements, moderating the final outcome for each pupil and ensuring that levels are ascribed.

Examinations are not, of course, the only form of assessment that occurs. Statutory assessment arrangements also involve teacher assessment of each pupil's achievements against an attainment target or level based on the pupil's school work within a Key Stage and the related test as marked by the class teacher.

In this context, assessment is not marked by an event, but more by a series of events. The process of building up evidence of each student's attainment over the course of a Key Stage is fundamental to good practice. Such evidence will be collated by teachers, with samples of pupils' work at different levels viewed by external moderators.

Assessment practices also vary in different schools or colleges. Common systems may be determined by a policy. Assessment policies might be based on curriculum areas or on departments developing their own systems based on agreed principles.

Teachers and curriculum managers might focus on a few questions, for example: how can any feedback be made purposeful and useful for assessment? How can previous experience be shared between different year groups and subject areas? How can the breadth of pupil achievement over time be celebrated, recorded and supported by evidence?

Once an assessment policy has been agreed, systems to support the process will follow. This might involve recording systems that can be adapted to individual needs, and ways of securing evidence to support assessment in more than one subject. Teachers and students can learn much from the process that could be shared with others.

If the purpose of assessment is to be both an indicator of achievement and a process that informs learning, the teacher is central to developing an understanding of procedures that enables the learner to progress. If educators were to assess in order to inform teaching and learning, more would be gained from the preparation and event, whatever the outcome.

Questions for discussion

The implementation of a knowledge-based curriculum, which is determined by the few to be delivered in a technical manner by the rest, has led to assessment as a system of accountability. There is a perception among those in high office that teachers are technicians, who are moving away from pedagogy towards a profession measured by their competence in filling the learner with knowledge rather than an understanding of how to learn. Practitioners can change this perception by demonstrating understanding of their practice. If assessment is to be a worthwhile educational activity, a range of new practices must be adopted. Consider:

1. How varied are the mechanisms for assessment in your classroom?
2. What abilities of the learner are you measuring? And why?
3. How do assessment outcomes inform practice?
4. As the technology of education is changing, how does this change impact on assessment?
5. Can the learner self-assess?
6. Once assessed, how are the outcomes communicated to the learner and others?

The art of report writing

In the opening chapter of *Matilda*, Roald Dahl describes how parents are sometimes of the impression that their child's achievements are at the level of genius. Dahl, perplexed by such 'twaddle', advises teachers to resort to foul play when writing reports. He suggests that teachers write that a child with limited ability is 'a total washout'. Dahl implies, as narrator, that if he were a teacher he would enjoy writing the 'end-of-term reports for the stinkers in his class'.

Dahl can pursue this line of thinking because his writing is the work of fiction not fact. School reports should of course be the latter. A report should assist the reader in developing a view that is helpful to the learner. So what should teachers put in reports and how useful are these reports in developing the child?

At this point, I would not deviate too far from Dahl's thinking. It is important for teachers to tell the truth, the helpful kind of truth that will assist the parent and child. Given that it is good practice to record every stage in a pupil's development, this evidence should be used a basis for reporting. Broad statements are nigh on useless in assisting the learner; specific guidance is needed. Use of databases is a good idea when individual records are kept on each pupil. However, be warned, that while statement banks can look impressive, parents trying to assess their child's ability will compare notes, at which point they become meaningless.

For teachers of minority subjects, who tend encounter the majority of the school in the course of a weekly or fortnightly timetable, providing detailed guidance and advice can be very difficult. Colleagues of mine in various schools have happily written reports on children who have never appeared in their classroom. How do these teachers ensure that they have something useful to say when writing a report ? The setting of precise targets for each lesson will assist with this process coupled with a simple tick-box method of recording. Targets can then be used to guide the report, these may also provide the hope and inspiration lacking in Dahl's comments.

Consider the child who, according to Dahl, is 'a total washout'. What could be said that would develop his or her learning? When writing or presenting such detail at parents' evening, a teacher has to take care not to insult either the child or the parent. For example, early years teachers who try to explain to parents how to do joined-up writing perhaps need guidance on joined-up thinking. Parents need to be advised on how a child can improve, not to be taught the content of the lesson. Equally, most parents, unlike those described by Dahl, do know whether their child needs to improve.

Presentation is all. If a parent and child are to benefit from the report they need to be able to read and understand it. The use of jargon is unhelpful, and spelling mistakes or poor grammar should also be avoided at all costs. As teachers approach report writing, perhaps they should imagine being the reader. While not wishing to read twaddle that might imply that their child is a genius, parents do anticipate something that informs, inspires and provides hope.

Questions for discussion

Teachers, parents and guardians are partners in the development of the whole child (DfES, 2004b). Decisions about the selection and location of a child's education are based on a report, which is often written in haste. In the context of workforce reform, teachers now have time to reflect and prepare meaningful reports. Consider:

1. How much time do you allocate to the preparation and writing of reports?
2. Are the reports meaningful to you and to others?
3. Do you discuss report writing with colleagues?
4. How do reports inform practice?

The public examination system is a bit like a lift

For reasons not worth reporting, I have recently become more aware of the wide range of lifts available. There are those that operate in two halves reaching either odd or even floors. These move quickly and silently to the top of high-rise buildings informing you that you are in the odd lift when you wanted to be in the even one.

The speed, lack of communication and clinical coldness of these lifts are in stark contrast to the open glass variety, found in shopping malls, which will give the shopper full sight of their destination. Such lifts often provide a running commentary that competes with the public address system announcing the ever increasing reductions on offer on each floor.

It struck me when I was in a lift of the silent, fast variety that this was not dissimilar to the experience of many pupils and students when they are trying to determine their potential. They are fed limited, often misleading, hard-to-translate information, possibly sending them heading towards an inappropriate destination.

The majority of learners are guided/constrained by the current mode of assessment for public examinations. We have to ask what this means in practice. What is an A? Is it an odd or even outcome? If it is in the context of a scale of assessment that has an A*, it could be considered odd. If it is in the context of A to E, it could be even. Confused? An A is not always as it seems. There is the possibility of further complication; should a student receive a B in a module of assessment, will there be any likelihood of them achieving an A at the end of the course? Would the teacher need to advise them to change direction in order to achieve the A, or to stay on the course to achieve a B, C or D? If an A is not achievable within the range of assessment, does the student stay with the B module or move to another programme?

I would imagine that the designers of lifts are fully engaged with their customers. The high-rise, silent variety are for high-rise, silent users. However, the majority of the human race would like to see and understand what is available before moving in a direction that leads them to an appropriate purchase. What if the A was set within clearly defined criteria understood by all – would the student be in a position to change course and attain a higher standard of performance? There are academic and vocational courses aplenty, and more are on their way. In the shopping mall of courses on offer to 14- to 19-year-olds, it would appear that the opportunities to reach the top are many.

I am sure that the majority of teachers and lecturers would like to present a clear and supportive framework to the learners in their classrooms. It is fairly clear that the need to guide students and pupils in an accessible and tangible manner is an aspect of learning that is often taken for granted by those who understand assessment criteria. It may be the case that students, teachers and lecturers require further guidance.

Is it clear what the possibilities are? Do they know whether to approach the odd or even lift? Ultimately, are the designers ready to provide a framework that will enable all users to understand how to reach the appropriate destination?

Questions for discussion

The use of technology as a means of communicating the organisational life is evident in most successful public and private enterprises. Through the application of technology, there is the opportunity for all schools and colleges to define and inform employers, parents and learners about examinations. Consider:

1. Do all learners understand the purpose and process of the examinations they sit?
2. Is there adequate support to inform learners about examination systems?
3. Are learners adequately prepared for examinations?
4. Do you need support in preparing learners for examinations?
5. Do you have access to the necessary information on examinations?
6. How can you alleviate the stress of examinations?

A stressed teacher will be less effective than a relaxed one

It's the end of term. Teachers are tired and just at the time when they need a break, they find they have 101 reports to finish, schemes of work to prepare and the partner has invited the family to stay for a few days over Christmas (which you know will extend to at least five). In addition, they are about to hit the bad parenting list as they have left it too late to purchase the latest Disney toy because Nemo and his friends have all left the tank and are making their way to their child's classmates' stockings.

Teachers are justified in being stressed about stress. Teaching is stressful, as the medical profession and car insurance companies will testify. The reality of teaching is that marking does not disappear, lessons need to be prepared and families also require a fair share of our time. What is the antidote to a busy professional life? Perhaps *Finding Nemo* can provide an answer. A key character in the film is Crush the turtle. Turtles live to 150 years old and, if Crush is to be believed, they have quite a life. Swimming, relaxing, generally enjoying the company of fellow turtles and generally chilling out are key characteristics of a turtle's lifestyle. Teachers have much to learn from this.

The bonus of a longer life is motivation for change in itself. There are also professional considerations: a healthy relaxed teacher is an effective teacher. If that Monday morning feeling continues through to Friday, teachers might be suffering from stress. Positive attitudes in the classroom are often based on how the teacher and students are feeling. A litmus test for teachers is to count the number of times you lose concentration during the day. In the same way that teachers notice problems in pupils when they lose concentration, the technique can apply to teachers. For those feeling stressed it is important to accept that this is not a personal problem or weakness. Be fair to yourself and try to recognise the symptoms.

When Nemo's father, Marlin, and his companion, Dory, are travelling through the southern ocean they ignore the shark's advice. By taking the quickest route over the coral, they encounter jellyfish that sting them with their dangerous venom and the outcome is pain and disillusionment. Marlin and Dory lose control, and Crush and his friends have to come to their rescue diverting briefly from being carried by the current towards the warmer waters in the north.

How many times do teachers behave in a similar fashion, ignoring good advice? It is quite something not to feel pressured by others, to enjoy getting on with people, including those we teach. Doctors tell us to exercise, go for a walk, drink in moderation and to eat the right foods. In a busy schedule, not taking a break, grabbing a sandwich lunch and drinking more than the odd glass of wine might seem appropriate. Recognise that the quickest route might prove to be the most painful when it could be far more enjoyable just to go with the flow. Teaching is not about seeking perfection. The new primary strategy tells us excellence can only be achieved through enjoyment, for the pupil and the teacher. As we approach the Christmas break, teachers need to give themselves a healthy dose of 'me time'. Learn from Crush, Marlin and Nemo – be healthy, find an ocean, go for a swim and have a great time.

Questions for discussion

As experts in the classroom, teachers work alongside a plethora of para- and multi-agency professionals. This level of support for the learner is changing the professional landscape in schools and colleges. The teacher is now the leading professional whose time is committed to the learner thus diminishing the stress created by utilitarian tasks. Consider:

1. Do you have the support you need to focus on the learners in your classroom?
2. How can teamwork decrease stress?
3. How relaxed are you?
4. Have you addressed your work and life balance?

Summary

Much of this chapter has focused on the classrooms of the future informed by the present and the past. As seen in early adopter schools, the school is to be a centre of a child's development embracing an agenda for change which focuses on the whole child. In this context, teachers have new choices on how to engage with learning and teaching. If teaching is to be a profession, it is time to ensure that the status of all teachers is recognised by all.

5 Arts

Introduction

This chapter provides an insight into my world as a music and expressive arts teacher. The columns describe positive teaching and learning experiences facilitated by collaborative colleagues in a variety of settings. All reflect an inclusive approach to music education which is now embedded in my approach to other professional contexts.

A different tune

Last month [October 2004], OfSTED completed a survey of instrumental tuition in 15 local authorities. The report found that more girls than boys received instrumental lessons and that there was evidence of gender stereotyping in the instruments studied. Nine times as many girls as boys learn the flute, twice as many boys as girls learn the trumpet and one and a half times as many girls as boys receive tuition.

The report also stated that the music services did not have sufficient systems for monitoring such patterns, or strategies to try to counter stereotyping. OfSTED concluded, quite rightly: 'the present pattern of choice of instruments is limiting some pupils' access to worthwhile and musically balanced ensemble experiences.'

There is a real need for pupils to be encouraged to perform on instruments of their choice and in a range of ensembles. The limitations set by local authorities and schools are determining the socio-economic profile of those that learn instruments.

Not every music centre is like this. In a recent paper featured in the *Westminster Studies in Education*, Stephanie Duarte, a Portuguese colleague, and I describe two music centres with members that include rugby-playing flautists and ballet-dancing trumpet players.

The research focuses on the Corsham Music Centre in Wiltshire, a community music centre and registered charity, and the International Music Centre in Lisbon, Portugal. Both offer free instrumental tuition to children and young people aged 5 to 25 and the opportunity to play in an ensemble as soon as the player produces a sound.

Members are encouraged to teach each other in a manner not dissimilar to the Victorian monitor system, reducing the cost of the provision while enhancing the abilities of the pupils.

The standard of performance is high, many members achieving grade 8 and above in the senior ensembles. Although the emphasis is on inclusion and participation, players have developed into successful musicians, performing in national orchestras and composing original works for stage and concert halls.

No child is excluded and no fees are charged to those who cannot contribute. The centres are run by volunteers who fundraise to buy instruments and music, pay for tuition and contribute to the cost of tours. The centres have toured to France, Germany, Rome, Madrid and Luxembourg and throughout the UK; members have also had the opportunity to perform with groups from America, Canada and Australia.

In contrast to the 15 local authorities in the OfSTED report, neither cost nor availability of instruments have been inhibitors to the recruitment and teaching of young people.

Many of the musicians opted for their particular instrument because of the appearance or sound it made, and for the sheer joy of performing. In Corsham, the trumpet section often features more girls than boys and for a number of years the principal flautists have been boys.

The centres in Corsham and Lisbon provide open access to all pupils wishing to play an instrument. This differs from the selection processes practised by LEAs [local education authorities]. As many boys as girls participate in the centres, and the musicians are representative of diverse socio-economic and educational backgrounds.

When asked why they joined, the children replied: 'You get to know people you would otherwise not meet, either because they're not at your own school or because they're not in your social circle'; 'There is a strong team feeling on trips and tours which is hard to experience elsewhere'; 'There is no rivalry in music.'

Why do Corsham and the Lisbon centres succeed where local authorities fail? Commitment in deed, as well as word, to the goal of providing access for all regardless of gender, ethnicity, disability or socio-economic background appears to be the answer. Often LEA-run music centres select students and ignore the inclusion agenda. But the Corsham and Lisbon centres sit outside local authority control and therefore are able to give open access to those wishing to join.

OfSTED's report diagnoses many of the malaises. But its suggested cures are too restrictive and could reinforce rather than reduce the problems. OfSTED recommend that music services become more integrated within the LEA. This, it believes, would ensure that staff understand and implement policies for inclusion, equality of access and equality of opportunity for all. However, in practice this would lead directors of music centres to more rhetoric that presents a complex and almost impossible framework for the delivery of inclusive education. OfSTED says that when selecting instruments, teachers should ensure that inappropriate gender stereotyping is challenged and that ways of tackling the gender imbalance in instrumental take-up are found. But this gives teachers responsibility over that of the pupil.

OfSTED wants music centres to use data on grades, both musical and academic, on relative poverty and so on. But this is counter-productive labelling, the very antithesis of the open-house, self-selection policy in Corsham and Lisbon.

Both OfSTED advice and LEA practice lack the spontaneity that links music to social development and invites all young people to participate in a musical community where friendships and confidence are deemed as important as the ability to play an instrument.

In Corsham and Lisbon, skills are developed through

teaching and guiding younger members. More skilled participants gain a deeper understanding of their own needs – particularly in intonation, aural perception, notation and ensemble proficiency.

Children with learning and physical disabilities are supported and stimulated by the group. Students from different nationalities, socio-economic backgrounds, abilities and a wide age range are able to combine their efforts to the common good of the community of music makers.

Why? As the music educator Isaac Stern said: 'Not to make "musicians" out of everyday performers, but more important, to make them educated, alert, caring inquiring young people, who by playing music feel a part of the connective tissue between what the mind of man has been able to devise and the creativity of music … in other words, become literate, and part of the culture of the whole world.'

Questions for discussion

Teachers have often demonstrated their commitment as civil and cultural educators responsible for developing the whole child. The extended school or community school is not a new concept. Many schools have a long history of an extended curriculum. Whether this encompasses the arts, sports, languages or technology, the learner is the beneficiary of teachers who 'go the extra mile' in order to provide opportunities for individuals to contribute to the collective good. Consider:

1. What is the range of opportunities provided by your school or college beyond the core curriculum?
2. Can your school or college enhance its curriculum beyond its current narrative?
3. Do learners understand the core value of education: to serve the common good?
4. How do you contribute to learning beyond the classroom?
5. What are the opportunities for the learner to demonstrate their skills?

Teachers can still make performers of their students

When the National Curriculum was introduced, music and drama were the first arts disciplines to suffer at the fate of the timetable. But in the school where I taught at the time, parents, pupils and several teacher colleagues supported the notion that music, dance and drama could be developed within the community.

Together we stuck with the idea; by 1994 the arts charity created out of a school music department in Wiltshire moved into what remained of a Victorian primary school building. Community-led and funded, the Arts Centre is now ten years old. Fortunate as we were to have WOMAD (World of Music, Arts and Dance) just two miles down the road, we invited performers from around the globe to perform and lead workshops. We performed alongside them in Bath as we busked together to raise funds to sustain ourselves and the centre. Music, dance, drama and art have been central to the community that at its height almost rivalled the neighbouring city of Bath.

I also taught in London in a drab uninspiring school building boldly named after Dame Peggy Ashcroft. A team of senior leaders had been brought together to create a new Key Stage 4 curriculum delivered over a nine-week period which facilitated sessions lasting a morning or afternoon. Over a period of three years, my colleagues and I worked with London Contemporary Dance, the Royal College of Art, WOMAD and Bournemouth Symphony Orchestra, to name just a few. This culminated in a presentation evening where the guest of honour was none other than Dame Peggy Ashcroft.

The performers were generous with their time, and the students and staff were genuinely excited by the sessions and truly immersed in the learning experience that went with them into the classroom.

Although the instruction given by a dancer to, 'look into the mirror and kick higher' was taken a little too literally as a pupil practised outside a shop window while waiting for his bus.

The experience of involving students from diverse social settings in the arts whether in school or the community moves beyond that of learning a skill. It reveals that through involvement in the arts, young people can experience inclusion in its fullest possible sense.

Through arts lessons, rehearsals or performances, students shed the negative aspects of their lives and develop the positive. Alongside friends and teachers they learn how to express themselves in different forms. They may not be outstanding as artists but the light that shines through their eyes is brighter than any perfected performance.

Gaining the skills to be involved is at the centre of these activities; the ability to talk and share the experience with others remains ever present in the social dimension of their lives. For educators and artists, the common aim of this experience is not to make artists out of each of our students but to make them feel part of the world.

Questions for discussion

Engagement in any learning activity will enhance and develop self-esteem. This can be achieved through a discipline or event when individual learning occurs. The majority of schools and colleges within the UK recognise the need to provide a range of group and individual learning activities that encourage learning. As you develop your practice, consider:

1. What activities encourage all students to learn?
2. How many of these attributes involve external agents: performers, educators, sportsmen and women?
3. Do learners have the opportunity to reflect on the activities in which they participate?
4. Can you increase the range of learners who participate in creative learning?

A few tips on how to face the music of the school performance

As the clock struck midnight I brought down my baton to begin a school windband rendition of 'Jesus Christ Superstar' in a French village hall. During the opening bars, Mary (bass clarinet) collapsed into her stand, followed by Neil (trombone), Claire (clarinet) and Michael (euphonium). I waved to my teacher colleagues for some assistance – they thought that I was seeking applause and waved back! By the closing bars half of the band was asleep. This was in my first year of teaching and I had much to learn about performing with pupils.

The majority of schools produce a public performance during the academic year, most in the coming weeks. Teachers need first to think about preparing the performance itself; and a word to the wise – make sure that your colleagues, and senior leadership team support the production. Many school events are made considerably more stressful by colleagues who find rehearsals noisy, inconvenient and disruptive to their daily performances in the classroom. Plan rehearsals, and add a few more just in case, check out your plan with staff a term in advance and ask for the key players in the staff room to join your production team. Spread the load, develop a team approach and other teachers will have fewer problems.

Regardless of the level of performance, the standard of hospitality will provide the baseline from which the school will be judged by the range of visitors who attend. When we visit a theatre or concert hall we expect that the event will be special; parents and friends will expect the same of a school.

The school needs a licence to perform, health and safety checks should be carried out and the local fire officer informed. Organisers need to think carefully about the presentation and content of programmes and tickets: acknowledgements are fine if everyone is included, but list names at your peril. I once had the pleasure of hosting a well-known media personality. Her first name could be spelt a number of ways – we got it wrong and she was frosty all evening.

There are many more things to consider: what is the purpose of the event? Has this been communicated to the appropriate audience? How many rooms/

chairs/tables will be required? Do staff require name badges? Are all notice boards used effectively to promote learning? Try not to miss out on the opportunity to sell your school. Has the caretaker been notified? Rooms will need to be cleaned before and after the event. Is the furniture in the right place? Who will be responsible for front of house – greeting visitors to the school? Are staff/pupils aware of the appropriate dress code?

Refreshments – have arrangements been made? Is the school site clear of rubbish? Does the school look good – are flowers, for instance, required? Microphones and amplification – do they work? Have car parking arrangements been agreed with police/school caretaker? Have governors, LEA officers and members of the senior leadership team been invited?

Having read all of the above teachers will possibly be thinking: 'Why get involved?' From my French tour, three of the four players are now teachers – through participating in performances they all gained in confidence and learnt many skills, including how to fall from a stage without breaking a leg.

Questions for discussion

Teaching can often be a performance whether it takes place in the classroom, concert hall or other setting. Planning what is effective and appropriate for all involved will benefit participants, performers and the audience. Such planning involves a range of pragmatic considerations. The introduction of workforce reform has increased the opportunities for the facilitation of these events with a team of adults, rather than an individual, managing all aspects of the performance. When you organise an event, consider:

1. How can the team assist with the planning and delivery of the event?
2. What will the event contribute to the school or college?
3. How will the event be of benefit to all participants?
4. What will the benefits of the event be to you?

Creative ideas can be found in the oddest places

I had the privilege of starting my career at a time when creativity and innovation were valued commodities in teaching. But many of those teachers new to the profession are a product of schools that have delivered the National Curriculum since 1988 under which the means of delivery is prescribed to meet the need to assess against school attainment targets.

The introduction of the National Curriculum led to a reduction in time available in the week for creative work in the majority of our schools. Music, art, dance and drama are placed on the periphery of the timetable. This is particularly the case in primary schools where the emphasis is on numeracy and literacy. In this context, teachers need to exercise fully their creative skills to develop a curriculum that excites and engages the minds of our learners.

Twelve years ago, while debating the curriculum, arts teachers were also developing ways to utilise what little time they had. In 1991, English Heritage offered teachers the use of their buildings for combined arts projects. A colleague, Jonathan Barnes, took up the invitation at Dover Castle and I led a project at Chiswick House. These projects were remarkably similar in their aim, which was to involve as many young people as possible in developing their artistic knowledge, understanding, skills and abilities in the context of the environment. Jonathan has since developed a national reputation for his creative approach to teaching. My 'Arts in the Environment' project took 15 teachers and nearly 500 pupils across Key Stages 2 and 3 into Chiswick House to dance, make music and create huge sculptures. On the day of the performance the result was outstanding. Pupils from diverse social and cultural backgrounds came together, performing in an environment quite different from those that they had previously experienced.

The project had begun with a visit to the house by year 7 pupils. The task was to explore and discuss the possibilities stimulated by the entrance, rooms and grounds. While the house was less than five miles from the school the majority of pupils did not know of its existence. From these discussions music, dance and drama teachers responded to planned classroom activities for the actual event held three months later. The teachers and pupils were struck by the dimensions of the building and its whiteness. Thus the music created was an aural representation of the shape of the entrance, with the grand stairs and balustrades. Dance was in keeping with the Georgian style, very controlled and repetitive but with flowing lines. The art was particularly impressive – large paper structures that were placed in the sculpture park created in the grounds.

As creative and expressive artists, pupils gained an experience at Chiswick House that would remain with them throughout their education. The level of stimulation the building provided inspired pupils to be remarkably creative. The investment? A timetable that was flexible, supportive staff and the freedom to engage with an environment that had been geographically close, but creatively at a distance from the pupils and teachers.

Questions for discussion

Creative opportunities are all around us. The environment is a natural stimulus for learning. Historical, modern and virtual settings can provide teachers with an infinite number of possibilities in which to engage the learner. Consider:

1. Can you identify creative opportunities in the environment in which you work?
2. How could you utilise the environment to stimulate learning?
3. What projects have you developed that encompass past, present and future settings?
4. How can you expand your knowledge of the environment and utilise this in the classroom?

Summary

Generations of learners have experienced the joy of engaging with the arts and the environment. Many of these activities have been made possible by the commitment of teachers to provide creative and educational opportunities through music, art, dance, drama and environmental history. These activities have taken the school curriculum to the community and its environment. These activities underpin the notion of the extended or community schools that engage teachers, parents and local community organisations in creating learning opportunities. The DfES Five Year Strategy (DfES, 2004d) encompasses many established ideas that have featured in this chapter. In working together, professionals and the community can extend the educational landscape as a stimulus and a contributor to learning. The key to success remains inclusion, of all learners, their families and friends.

Questions for discussion

1. Are you familiar with the government's extended school agenda?
2. Does your school or college have an extended curriculum?
3. How is the extended curriculum evaluated?
4. How inclusive of others – parents, community and all pupils – is the extended curriculum?
5. How can your extended curriculum encourage the disaffected, alienated learner to engage in learning?
6. What are the professional development needs of those engaged in the management and delivery of the extended school?

6 Professional development

Introduction

All schools, colleges and higher education institutions (HEIs) have the potential to create an effective learning environment. If teachers and learners are to be effective in these environments, teachers need to be learners. In order for the learning community to progress teachers, as reflective practitioners and learners, will engage in professional development. The importance of professional development cannot be overstated.

From initial training to educational leadership and beyond, professional development is the core of a teacher's learning and can be manifest in many forms. The columns provide illustrative commentary of professional development in practice.

Trainee teachers need qualified and devoted mentors

When I first moved into higher education as a teacher educator, I was inevitably required to observe trainees delivering lessons. As unqualified teachers, they were supported by an experienced mentor who was qualified to teach.

My first observation was memorable for a number of reasons. The lesson was year 9 science, the trainee was a very nervous biochemist who had left the laboratory to train as a teacher. This was the second week of his practice and the fourth week of the school term. The Bunsen burners were out, as the experiment was the assumed safe testing for acids and alkalis. At the back of the room was the experienced mentor. Having been introduced, I sat to one side. A technician was busy setting up the test tubes. Following clear instructions the pupils moved to their benches. Within seconds, they turned the classroom into a battle zone with broken glass and flaming burners. The trainee was mortified, the mentor was busy with his own work, against all advice I intervened. In doing so, I commented on how the head teacher would feel disappointed at their behaviour. This led to a few sighs of embarrassment, as the mentor was the head teacher! Having restored the class to order, the trainee was able to continue with the lesson, at the end of which I talked to the head teacher.

Apparently, during the previous term the caretaker had left, the school needed painting and the head had rolled up his sleeves and spent much of the summer painting. He was very proud of his handiwork and took me to the places that he had been finishing while the trainee had been 'teaching' his classes. What he failed to recognise was a perceived loss of role by the pupils and the inevitable lack of support for the trainee.

There is an increasing number of unqualified teachers and trainees in schools without the support of an experienced mentor. Where and how do they begin?

Consider the science trainee. From the outset, he needed to understand the curriculum, which encompasses all sciences; he had limited access to such materials. His curriculum and lesson plans should have been based on a clear understanding of the National Curriculum and schemes of work. In addition, assessment of processes and outcomes was underdeveloped in the school and left the trainee feeling completely lost.

As witnessed during the lesson, behaviour management is absolutely crucial to effective teaching. A trainee needs guidance which takes time and patience for all involved. Curriculum, assessment and behaviour are just three elements of the role of the teacher, and there is much more for the unqualified teacher to consider that cannot be captured in a few words.

All of the above would be daunting for any professional, but for those without any significant level of training prior to entering the classroom the importance of support from experienced teachers is vital.

Teaching should be guided and led by trained professionals. There needs to be space in the timetable and a physical space with supporting material, access to a computer and in-school training. At the start of a career, time needs to be set aside for talking, listening and enjoying being a teacher.

Questions for discussion

Teaching is a profession, which is underpinned by theory and demonstrated in practice. The practice of teaching involves the participation of learners. As a teacher develops, learners are also provided with an opportunity to develop. This relationship is immensely complicated yet the education and training of teachers in the classroom is often left to chance. Where professional development is taking place, it generally starts with the mentoring of trainees, which also requires an expertise underpinned by theory. Higher education institutions are able to facilitate the training of mentors as a prerequisite to planning a trainee's time in schools and colleges. The introduction of employment-based routes into teaching emphasises the importance of mentor training for all teachers engaged in the training of other teachers. Consider:

1. What are the training opportunities for mentors in your school or college?
2. How are the differing routes into teaching managed in your school or college?
3. Do all mentors have an understanding of their trainees' needs?
4. What are your partnership arrangements with local higher education institutions?
5. Do these partnerships facilitate good practice? How can these be improved?

How to give newly qualified teachers a good start

At this time in the academic year many students are preparing for their new roles as teachers. They are full of enthusiasm and commitment, ready to become professional practitioners and to work alongside those with the expertise and experience to guide them as they join the teaching workforce. Yet staff retention remains a critical issue in most schools and local education authorities.

What do these new practitioners need in preparation for their posts? They will be aware from the job description and person specification of what is required of the post holder. They will also need to know their position within the school structure. Who will be their line manager? Who is in their team? When and how will they be introduced to all staff? In my experience, a low-key introduction on a one-to-one basis is often preferable to a grand entrance.

Ideally, relevant documentation should be prepared for the interview so the new appointee can take away further details. Following the appointment, the manager can arrange times for the appointee to visit the school and department to meet new colleagues and pupils. The appointee will also need to be made aware of the school and department aims through relevant documentation, possibly a staff handbook. This might contain: staff, room and class lists, policies, school calendar, map, and health and safety details. This would be an invaluable resource for any new appointee, and others too. Schemes of work and the timetable should be made available well in advance of the first day of term, as should reporting and assessment procedures.

Effective induction will need to be both planned and flexible, identifying the training, development and personal needs of the new appointees. Negotiation is central to this process: a new colleague will need to agree the most appropriate personal and professional support in a climate of mutual respect. This works in schools with an open environment where the needs of others are respected. There are a number of activities that will help new appointees and long-term staff, such as job-shadowing and observation, which lay the foundation for reflective practice.

The professional development coordinator has an important role to play in the induction of newly qualified teachers. A mentor could provide support for any new colleague – release time for the staff involved. The money for any supply cover should be available. This might encourage staff to become involved in the induction activities, thus promoting the school as a learning environment.

In addition to professional matters an employer has a duty of care. Senior leaders have a responsibility to assist with accommodation, transport and creating a social environment for newly qualified teachers. Many local authorities provide such support and others should learn from this good practice. At a glance it is easy to recognise those teachers who have been supported during the first weeks and months of their new post. They are ones who stay with the school or local education authority. As with most events in life, planning and preparation is good investment for the future.

Questions for discussion

'Firsts' are memorable occasions, the first day in a new post being no exception. For the new appointee, there is much to absorb – schools and colleges are complex organisations. At this time support will be available through professional development activities. As the workforce in schools and colleges expands, mentors, coaches and buddies will help to induct the new post holder. Such systems are commonplace within the private sector and could easily be adopted within educational settings. Consider:

1. Are new post holders provided with the information they require prior to taking up the post?
2. Do you have a mentor or buddy system for all staff?
3. What support and information systems are in place for new post holders in your school or college?
4. How do these systems relate to and reward ongoing professional development experienced prior to the post holder joining your school or college?

Much more thought should be given to planning staff training days

As a teacher who has experienced many 'Baker days' that have left me feeling uninspired and in some cases desperate, I have often wondered how much thought is given to such events. At least five days a year are given over to staff development in the form of in-service education and training (Inset) – such days need careful planning, much the same as a good teacher would apply to the curriculum they deliver to their pupils.

A colleague of mine, James Learmonth, was an advocate of schools working in partnership with local education authorities and higher education institutions to create relevant training that would have a positive impact on practice. However, having talked to a number of very busy head teachers, I fear that planning Inset is not seen as a priority.

As professionals, teachers should view their place of work as a place of learning. Within the framework of continuing professional development, self-development and staff development are prerequisites for effective management and effective schools. Within this context, planning for Inset will require several months of review and consultation.

Perhaps a way of developing a meaningful Inset programme might be a team representing the views of all staff. Once drafted, the programme could be circulated and views sought from colleagues on appropriate approaches to each element. The final details would reflect staff needs and concerns. These should relate directly to school, teacher and pupil needs. Inset is only part of the process of developing, implementing and reviewing the raising of achievement, but should be placed in the context of practice.

Having agreed on the focus, aims and objectives, thought is needed on how to present the material. The style, content and relevance of Inset should acknowledge the importance of varied teaching and learning styles in a practical sense. Time should be given to reflect individually and in groups and relevant information should be circulated in advance to enable staff to consider their position in relation to important policies and practice. It should be unlike one experience I shared with colleagues in a secondary school in the West

Country, when the consultant insisted that there was only one approach to assessment – his. It is important to recognise that staff need to feel supported and confident that their contribution will be valued.

There is a tendency for school leaders to use the valuable time given to Inset for the presentation of information. However, long lists or meaningless prose are not appreciated by staff. I recently had to deliver a list of 136 programmes, destined to have a soporific effect on the 250 staff present. Faced with this challenge, the team decided to adapt television and film themes, and the list appeared on a large screen in a style based on the first 10 minutes of *Star Wars*.

Location is important. It is sometimes beneficial to use an off-site venue to generate an atmosphere in which teachers can feel relaxed.

Inset planning teams have a huge responsibility to inspire through events that lead to sustainable outcomes for pupils and teachers.

Questions for discussion

The future of schools and colleges is being determined within a framework of change. Change management is now embedded in a teacher's practice which is underpinned by changes that are global, environmental, technological and social. These take the learner and teacher to a far different place than that experienced in the previous 140 years of national schooling. Practitioners are being taken out of their comfort zone and into new areas that might prove to be difficult to recognise. Professional development can provide a framework to support practitioners as they engage with these changes. Consider:

1. How relevant is Inset to the future development of professional teachers within your school or college?
2. Is Inset planned, delivered and monitored in a meaningful way?
3. What are the motivating features of the professional development activities that engage all practitioners?
4. How can information be communicated on professional development activities? Is there a central location for such information?

Make provision for continuing professional development – a space to grow

A few years ago, I was invited to present my thoughts on educational management to the staff of a well -known grammar school. When the day arrived, I approached the entrance hall with trepidation, thinking, as a former secondary modern pupil, I would find the experience to be culturally challenging.

The building was old, practical and impressively clean. I was led to the head teacher's study, which in itself had an air of academic endeavour. The walls were lined with books and the inevitable National Curriculum folders, head's legal guide and other such information. The importance of knowledge transferred through the written word was self-evident.

Leaving the study, I was taken to the staff library, where the session was to be held. As expected, there were a significant number of books that ranged from subject-based material to management texts and a more eclectic collection of literary classics. The library had the feeling of those found in the best-resourced higher education institutions. It was evident that the staff enjoyed participating in reading and discussion.

Not all schools or colleges have such a facility, yet it is my belief that all teachers and lecturers should have access to the written word that will help to guide and inspire. There must have been some point in each teacher's career when reading about educational issues was a pleasure. When did this change? Is it that there is not the availability of space, time and suitable texts? I am sure that this is the reasoning expressed by some colleagues.

However, in other learned communities such as hospitals, accountancy firms, law practices and the church there are spaces for the collection of books and other supporting materials. So why do schools and colleges have such limited provision for staff?

There may be a perception of a lack of interest in such matters. I have recently completed a text on financial management in schools in collaboration with a local secondary school head teacher, who gave the impression that he was 'out of the ordinary' in that he regularly read about educational matters. What if schools and colleges were to invest in creating the space and time for professional development through publications? Would this raise standards and levels of achievement? As this does not happen, it would be difficult to provide the evidence to support this argument.

Many teachers are given the opportunity to attend courses at higher education institutions, where they are fully engaged in the reading of educational literature. In this context, much is learnt, shared and celebrated in a supportive environment.

Returning to the grammar school and its study and staff library, what did this contribute to the ethos and general sense of well-being within the school? These were quiet, calm places where staff could read, reflect and consider their practice. They were also places where staff could develop, professionally and personally.

The staff looked relaxed during my time with them. They were also able to discuss issues in an informed manner, with confidence in front of their colleagues, such was the sense of respect for knowledge.

Questions for discussion

The continuing development of professional practice has a place in the lives of all teachers. Reflective practice will enhance the educational experience of teachers and learners. Schools and colleges that provide a space in which professionals can grow are committing to the principle of a learning community. Where this happens is often left to chance; libraries, computers, information boards and other resources can locate the teacher within their own extended place for learning. Consider:

1. What opportunities are there for you to reflect on practice? Is there space and time?
2. Do you engage in professional dialogue that will help you to develop your knowledge, skills and understanding as a reflective practitioner?
3. Is there investment in resources that facilitate professional development?
4. How will this book and others inform your practice?

Everyone should consider further study for themselves

Many of you will know of staff, friends and colleagues who have entered teaching or learning support via what is termed a non-traditional route. This means those who did not have the opportunity to complete GCSE or A level programmes for a variety of reasons.

Since 2000, foundation degrees have been developed by HE [higher education] and FE [further education] institutions to provide an opportunity for people who are working to develop their professional understanding, knowledge and key skills while remaining at work. The principal aims of such programmes are to widen access into higher education.

In my *Professional Development in Schools Manual* (Blandford, 2004a), I describe the possibilities offered by work-based foundation degrees which provide lifelong learning opportunities for all para-professionals who work in a school, college or HE environment.

Head teachers might wish to consider what foundation degrees could provide for their staff. A possibility could be courses for learning assistants, often those without traditional A level qualifications, but who have considerable experience of working in the fields of education and/or childcare. Several local education authorities now have professional development programmes for learning and teaching assistants that include qualifications. Within the institutions offering such programmes, there are a range of access or orientation courses.

For many learning assistants the question is: why embark on such a programme? I think that those involved can speak for themselves.

Having left school at 15, Jane embarked on a career that included shop and factory work. Following the birth of her children she concentrated on running the home. Jane worked in the local primary school on a voluntary basis, assisting with reading and art. The local authority ran a programme to develop the skills of the volunteers; this led Jane to an access programme and foundation degree. This year, Jane graduated with first-class honours in childhood studies, and is now working towards qualified teacher status. She continues to work in the same school where she began as a volunteer seven years ago. Next year she will have responsibility for a class and other para-professionals who are about to embark on an access programme.

The benefits to the school have been tremendous. Jane lives locally and is part of the community; her knowledge of those attending the school is boundless. Jane also has a wealth of understanding that underpins her practice in the classroom. Her courses have included behaviour management, curriculum development and special educational needs, all relevant to effective classroom practice.

Jane is a great role model. Having left school with few qualifications, she now has a degree and can inspire those she teaches. She has also been invited to attend LEA training programmes to contribute to the professional development of other parents and members of the community who want to gain an education while sharing their skills and knowledge with the next generation of learners.

Questions for discussion

The remodelled workforce in schools and colleges is a new agenda for practitioners. Teachers are to become leaders and managers of learning supported by a range of expertise. As mentioned, the notion of the self-managed network might be worthy of further consideration to develop practitioners, who will work in partnership with other agencies, creating a network of learners that can inform and develop practice. With knowledge of their subject matter and pedagogy, graduates are able to develop the skills and competences to guide and support learners with an understanding of the social and cultural dimensions of education. This places teachers within a continuum of lifelong learning from initial education through to advanced practice and qualifications. Consider:

1. Are you motivated to learn?
2. Do you invest time in your own professional development?
3. Do you participate in a learning network that facilitates your professional development?
4. How does your professional development impact on your practice?

Summary

Teachers who are educated and trained contribute to the economic, social and cultural aspects of the knowledge society. In practice, teachers work with information, knowledge and technology. They work with people who are citizens living in a global society. As educators who engage with others, teachers are developing in new ways; they are becoming self-managed networkers. It is axiomatic that professional development of self and others is located within the practice and experience of a teacher's professional life.

7 Futures

Introduction

In September 2003 a unique agreement was struck between unions and government agencies to secure improved working conditions for teachers (DfES, 2003a). This has led to the remodelling of schools where a teacher's practice will focus on learning with less emphasis on administrative and support tasks. They and their teams will create places and spaces for teaching and learning. In these new settings teachers will be the facilitators of knowledge enabling learners to access and discover learning in a variety of forms. Set within the context of future social, economic, technological and educational change, teachers will accommodate changes as a matter of course. Change management will continue to be a normal part of a professional's life.

To enable change to occur within a secure, comfortable place, the direction of schools within a knowledge society will need to be transparent to all. The sharing of experience and learning will be commonplace whereby teachers will be the decision-makers both informing and contributing to the change. This is of benefit to all where time is made available for reflection, development, delivery and evaluation of learning. Thus a teacher's life is to become more attractive to graduates from all disciplines; such is the vision, met in part by those Pathfinder schools and early adopters. This chapter will provide a balance between this expectation and other initiatives that have taken place in the 'real' world.

Differences in educational provision in schools and FE colleges

To some, a zebra might look like a horse and to others the differences might appear to be so great that it is difficult to consider them as genetically related in any way. However, as the textbooks tell us, the zebra belongs to the same family as horses and ponies.

The classification of the current and proposed educational provision for 14- to 19-year-olds is the equivalent of bringing together zebras and horses. The form the provision takes has a family likeness, but we should recognise the stripes when we see them.

Being of compulsory school age, the majority of 14- to 16-year-olds are taught in schools. Most people would identify with schools as places which provided them with a particular type of learning experience.

The order and structure of the school is planned according to the perceived needs of the majority: lessons of a given length, teachers trained according to the government's standards to deliver a curriculum that has been planned by a committee. Schools are domesticated places where, in the moral sense, a teacher *in loco parentis* has responsibilities for the pupils in their care. Inevitably, there is an emphasis on nurturing and caring for the needs of the individual in an environment that is secure and predictable. In schools the duty of care is as significant as teaching.

In contrast, further education college practitioners are as different as the many creatures that mix together on the plains of east Africa. From the smallest to the largest, FE colleges offer programmes which are many and varied, be they trade-based, academic or at the level of basic needs. Hairdressers and accountants come together to deliver courses to generations of post-compulsory learners from 16 to 80.

To facilitate this process, the FE environment provides a flexible framework: sessions are delivered day and night. In an effort to ensure quality of learning and teaching, all FE lecturers are now trained to meet the standards set by the Further Education National Training Organisation.

In my recent visits to a number of sites across the South-East of England, it is clear that further education colleges are caring and secure environments. However, lecturers are not *in loco parentis*, students are self-selecting; the uniform is varied, not of a single colour.

An FE student is a very different beast to a pupil. At college, the student is responsible for ensuring that they attend the course – the alternative is failure rather than a series of measures set by a senior member of staff. Behaviour is determined by the need to learn. If the behaviour is unacceptable the student can be asked to leave the course.

The conditions of service for a lecturer are outcome-driven; students are taught to succeed in courses and disciplines that they may have failed at school. Further education lecturers have the highest proportion of teaching hours in the education family; they earn their stripes.

Culturally, educationally and socially diverse, it will be interesting to see what happens when the horses and zebras of the education family are classified as one.

Questions for discussion

Government policies shape society, yet some might argue that the authors of each policy fail to influence each other. A curriculum that extends beyond compulsory education is a sound proposition. Work-based learning will continue to grow as small and medium-sized enterprises emulate larger organisations and the public sector workforce becomes more educationally aware. How this will be structured and systematised remains a subject for debate. In the meantime, there is an opportunity for schools and colleges to network and develop a curriculum for themselves. Consider:

1. How do schools and colleges communicate? Are networks in place?
2. What would be a common curriculum for 14–19, 19–26, 26–40 and over 40 year olds?
3. How can practice influence policy?
4. Who will be responsible for the delivery of the curriculum?

Recruit people to the profession

Remember *Back to the Future*? The film that was based on the creation of a machine that looked like a mid-1960s racing car, yet was able to take a young man back to the time his parents met. He could have changed the future by marrying his own mother. The idea was creative and for some inspirational. The story ended as the mother and father were graduating from high school and were reunited at the dance.

At this point in the school and college year, head teachers and principals are considering how to attract the best teachers and lecturers to their institutions. There have been those that have offered a range of incentives from a weekly massage to downtime for shopping, while others have tried to entice applicants by describing the staff in an exciting and vivid manner. Have any of these marketing techniques worked? Are there huge numbers of graduates and mature people wanting to teach? The volume of vacancies in the recruitment pages appears to state otherwise.

The idea of going back in order to influence the future is one that some might find appealing. Some might consider why they became a teacher; others might be reflecting why not. Yet teaching has the potential to affect the lives of the current school and college generation.

In the *Guardian's* reporting of the Teaching Awards 2003, there were many accounts of how teachers influenced the lives of the learners. The headlines were themselves inspirational: 'Born to Teach', 'Engage the Young' and 'Children's Champion'. There is a dedicated workforce that continues to inspire and motivate the learners in their classrooms. Indeed Ted Wragg commented that 'a whole recruiting campaign should be built around the winners of this year's awards.' Why seek alternative means of attracting staff when the exemplification of good practice through heartfelt accounts could do the job?

For anyone who might be considering teaching as a career, there are a number of routes – seventeen and a half at the last count. Look at the Teacher Training Agency website and you will be dazzled by the plethora of programmes: part-time, full-time, award-bearing, non-award bearing via higher education or employment-based. A route that will take you through the 42 standards leading to qualified teacher status is there for you. Revisit the account of the 2003

Teaching Awards and I hope that this will inspire you. As the regional finalists of 2003 reported, 'teaching exceeded their original expectations, and they were genuinely surprised and moved by the difference they seemed to make for youngsters' lives.'

Once recruited the next challenge is to retain staff. Teachers are professionals who have spent time refining their craft. Professional standing in the community is important – and how this happens is often a reflection on the leadership of the school.

The opportunity to develop is of paramount importance to the new teacher. Teaching should not be considered as a life of mundane repetition of the National Curriculum. As in other professions, further academic awards and professional development have a place. There is scope for change and development.

Questions for discussion

Teaching is a profession of over 400,000 people in the UK. It is a profession that continues to attract 14,000 recruits on an annual basis. The number of training routes into teaching reflects the government's recognition that people enter the profession at different points in their lives and the retention of teachers is problematic. Teach First is a recent innovation, where first-class graduates from Russell Group universities are offered a package of teaching and business training; within this programme, participants gain qualified teacher status and MBA credits. The programme began in London and, being city-based, participants are placed in challenging schools which have reported on the success of the programme. Participants are committed professionals and reflect the norm in teacher education – it is this professionalism which is at the heart of the remodelling agenda. Consider:

1. What are the professional characteristics of teaching?
2. Has teaching developed within the context of a knowledge society?
3. How can established teachers contribute to the retention of staff?
4. Why is teaching exciting and rewarding?
5. How can teachers attract graduates to the profession?
6. Can technology modernise the profession?

Increased use of computers has had a limited impact on learning

Travelling by train in the South-East of England can be quite tortuous given the ages of carriages and the varying interpretations of the timetable. On many journeys, I've observed that the passengers who seem to have the best coping mechanisms for such journeys are those that interact with various forms of mobile technology. In particular, teenage boys appear to be good with quite advanced equipment – which is odd considering that we often read that boys are not very good at interacting with learning in the classroom.

Many teachers work in classrooms far older than the average rolling stock. Yet we have moved a long way from slates, Banda machines and collators. Most schools have a whiteboard and computer suites. The majority of teachers are now computer literate and our students enjoy access to a range of technologies at home and in school.

Have levels of attainment been enhanced by technology? A significant number of government initiatives have been designed to encourage the effective use of information technology as an aid to learning. Yet as the recent report by

Becta, the government's ICT [information and communications technology] agency, clearly states, while there have been a considerable increases in the number of computers in classrooms, the impact on learning and teaching is minimal. We have to ask why. Perhaps the answer is the educational equivalent of 'leaves on the line' – if the fundamentals remain the same, information technology may have limited impact.

Supporters of the most recent government initiative to place interactive whiteboards in classrooms claim that this will change learning and teaching as we know them. My expert colleagues tell me that the preferred set-up is a back-projected wireless model, though whether this refers to the teacher I can only hazard a guess. What does a whiteboard offer? Instant access to the Internet, with a plethora of resources and ideas and the means to record each lesson as it happens. Associated technology can record and collate pupil assessments by video, in writing and on databases.

There is also the potential to link the screen to notebooks, an amazing piece of technology that is able to record handwritten notes alongside those issued by the teacher through a wireless connection direct to each student. A number of technology schools have issued notebooks to all classes; the results (especially with boys) have been dramatic.

The messages are clear: if the technology is here to stay teachers must get to grips with the gizmos and pedagogy. My colleagues at Canterbury Christ Church University College have adopted a staged approach to the introduction of whiteboards. Rather than using government funds for equipment alone, we introduced training sessions for students and teachers. The response has been constructive.

Staff now plan lessons in order to engage students through interacting with technology. The technology is not just a means of communication; it is applied to enhance learning. I would advocate this approach in schools. Training sessions led by educational experts who can adapt and develop learning to respond to the changing technology are more useful than an extra whiteboard used for communication only.

Before we get too excited and jump onto the train hoping to wirelessly link our laptops to whiteboards and transmit our lessons across the globe, perhaps we should reflect on prevailing practice and ponder 'why do trains fail to run on time?'

Questions for discussion

Through remodelling, the infrastructure that supports education is moving to a new dimension. Networking is critical to learning systems and structures. A school or college that is not networked is not synchronised with the predominant ideology underpinning business and public sector organisations. Technology is networked, the World Wide Web being the greatest channel for networking. The creation of the Internet also impacted on the way and what we learn; access for information has never been easier. However, as research has shown, the impact on learning has been minimal. It seems that Internet users have a limited capacity to embrace what is on offer and learn. The key is pedagogy – learning and teaching. Consider:

Questions for discussion *continued*

1. How is technology used in your school or college?
2. Are you trained in the use of technology?
3. Can technology alone enhance learning?
4. How can pedagogy underpin the application of technology?
5. How can technology contribute to workforce reform?

Is remodelling the National Curriculum the way forward?

Ten years ago, having moved to a new school and locality, I was introduced to a number of new friends. I immediately recognised their voices; they belonged to the Creature Comfort penguins then used to promote an electricity board. Aardman Productions had used their friends to provide the inspiration and voices for the plasticine models. Such was the success of the adverts that the animated film production company has gone on to win several international awards, including two Oscars.

The same schools were just coming to terms with the introduction of the National Curriculum. The original version, created by teams of teachers and civil servants across the land, and presented in a number of A4 binders, was sent to all maintained primary and secondary schools in England and Wales. Each subject featured a number of attainment targets which were to assist the teacher in determining the lesson content. Each target was referenced against a level. Pupils were graded regardless of age.

We are all aware of what happened next: changes were recommended, implemented and reviewed, followed by further recommendations and review. The current version can be found in a single document with fewer, less explicit attainment targets. In parallel to several variations, national literacy and numeracy strategies were introduced and the national examination system changed.

Meanwhile, Aardman had stuck with the plasticine and created Wallace and Grommit, *Chicken Run* and other Creature Comforts. Yet the voices stayed with them.

The public liked what they saw, as evidenced by the company's success.

The National Curriculum has not been received with such enthusiasm. Parents, pupils and teachers remain passive recipients of a knowledge-driven curriculum. Creativity and individual development have been lost to the delivery of a prescribed amount of reading, writing and mathematics based on schemes of work that may not relate to the individual learner.

During the next 18 months, the model of delivering the National Curriculum is to be remodelled through the re-engineering of schools. Teachers will now manage a team of learning assistants led by a higher-level assistant. It will be the responsibility of the team to carry out the more mundane administrative tasks. The team will also assist the teacher in the delivery of the national literacy, numeracy and behaviour strategies.

Funding for this venture has yet to be agreed by local authorities through the Schools Forum working in partnership with all maintained schools. Further training for teachers is planned to facilitate the management of assistants in the classroom. Initial teacher training programmes will also be modified.

All this will take time, patience and professionalism. Perhaps those responsible for the remodelling can learn from Aardman. They continue to create programmes using the trademark ingredients of a lump of plasticine, simple backdrops and the voices of their friends. As with the many messages presented in ten-minute animations, this appears to be philosophically sound without being too profound.

Questions for discussion

There is a perception among policy-makers that the technology of teaching has remained the same over the last 140 years. Clearly this is not so. The place of learning might be Victorian but the mode of learning is located in the twenty-first century. In the majority of

▶

Questions for discussion continued

schools and colleges, teachers are graduates, masters of their craft with an understanding of theory and practice. Learners are also beginning to present at different ages, with many retired people now joining learning sets through the University of the Third Age. As this wide range of learners embark on a voyage of discovery, the resources to support engagement with learning are also changing, driven by technology and a greater understanding of how humans learn. At the core of the expansion of the knowledge society is learning and teaching, a relationship where the teacher engages learners whose ability to learn is a reflection in part of the teacher's ability to teach. Consider:

1. What are the core elements of teaching and learning that remain constant in a changing world?
2. How do teachers engage with change?
3. Do you have the skills, knowledge and resources that will enable you to participate?
4. What will be your role in 2025?
5. How can you shape the future?

Remodelling the workforce – how to make best use of extra staff

One of the rituals to be experienced by teachers in schools and colleges is the compulsory training days normally held in the first week of the academic year. Since the first 'Baker days' were introduced by the then Education Secretary, Kenneth Baker, in 1985, a minimum of five training days have been set aside for teachers in mainstream schools. These are run for a variety of reasons and provide the opportunity for teachers to discuss how to implement national, regional and local policies that have been produced at the loss of several forests during the last 25 years.

Given the emphasis in current thinking on learning and teaching, it would seem appropriate that teachers are provided with the opportunity to recharge their thinking by reflecting on the government's plans to remodel the school workforce. It has taken several summers and lots of paper to generate a plan that is to unburden teachers, who have been beset by additional administrative tasks since the 1988 Education Reform Act and the start of the National Curriculum.

Additional staff are being employed to stand by the photocopier, collect dinner money, take the register, provide cover for absentee teachers and provide additional support in the classroom.

While head teachers and their staff are now in the enviable position of having additional help, they are also faced with the problem of how to fully utilise the remodelled workforce. As head teachers tackle this issue, many of the recent training days will have focused on creating and implementing policies on how best to manage the workforce.

Once the workforce development plan has started, the next step is to ensure that there is appropriate follow-up. An action plan is the link between training and follow-up. It is the implementation process that links new learning to practice in the school and classroom. A good

action plan needs to give detailed consideration not only to the intended innovation, but also to the strategy that will be employed to implement it. The process of planning is often more important than the plan. In terms of the innovation itself, the action plan might address a range of questions including who will benefit from a remodelled workforce: pupils/students, colleagues? What will the costs be for those affected? Will additional resources be required to monitor the additional resources?

Once the workforce remodelling agenda has been agreed at the local level, it is also worth considering: is the change easy to communicate to those concerned and will they see its purpose? If this is not agreed, will it be possible to adapt what is intended to suit specific circumstances? Whose support will be needed? Will key people have a sense of ownership of the change?

Given the opportunities that exist with the remodelled workforce, it is time for all involved to train their own staff. This is where 20 years of Baker days, over one-third of a year of training, has led. If teachers do not work this one out for themselves those hard-working civil servants will do it for them.

Questions for discussion

All schools and colleges are different – there is no single blueprint for a successful school. Knowing the direction of the school or college as expressed in its vision will enable future practice and frame the wider workforce to participate with a shared sense of purpose. Inevitably, remodelling leads to the restructuring of schools and colleges. It is the community that should feel empowered to tackle the key issues that arise in the most appropriate way. Consider:

1. Do all members of the community have a shared understanding of the vision of the school or college?
2. How does the vision inform practice?
3. How does the vision facilitate change?
4. Does the vision have a life beyond 2010?
5. Where will the school or college be in 2025?

A new curriculum geared to individual needs

Listening to Sir Peter Maxwell-Davies describing the difficulties that audiences and performers had when engaging with 'modern' music during the middle of the last century caused me to reflect on the similarities with those who now engage with new methods of teaching. Maxwell-Davies explained that with the loss of the familiar structure and tonality of music, performers and listeners found it difficult to determine the nature and meaning of the pieces they were performing or hearing.

Similarly the nature of learning and teaching is changing – teachers are being encouraged to design a curriculum to meet the individual needs of the learner. Individual learning places the teacher at the centre not of a single model, but 20 to 30 models of learning, depending on the size of the class. To devise a curriculum that responds to individual learning needs requires detailed knowledge of the subject matter and a clear understanding of the pedagogy required. Here we lose the familiar structure of the curriculum that takes the learner through repeated patterns, much the same as the modern composers of the twentieth century lost the regularity of the four-bar phrase.

Neither learning nor music happens in isolation; the environment has a major impact on individuals engaged in either activity. Where schools can be re-engineered to give room to the broader, more varied curriculum that accommodates the academic, social and vocational needs of individuals, there is every opportunity that the learner will achieve. However, if the physical structure of the school prevents the learner or teacher from achieving the aims and objectives of the curriculum, little will be gained from any new initiative.

Notwithstanding the need for many schools to be rebuilt, there is the capacity for the majority to be refurbished in order to accommodate the new curriculum. The time is here for architects and teachers to discuss the redesign of schools.

Beyond this, staff will need to be trained to develop the appropriate skills. Teachers know that competencies can become obsolete; however, educators must produce something that is strong enough to achieve a balanced understanding of individual learners.

Teachers are aware of the increase in the impact of personal computers on the learner. The Internet provides a model for individual learning. However, computers can be isolating.

The social element of schools that prepares learners for society remains constant through the changes that challenge our thoughts. Maxwell-Davies also placed an emphasis on the social importance of music. It can provide the opportunity for people to interact. Irrespective of curriculum content or style of delivery, there is an ethical, values-led purpose to education. As we move into the next dimension of curriculum development, the importance of retaining the integrity and professional standing of education remains central to all our endeavours as learners and teachers.

Questions for discussion

Individual learning plans, where the learner is guided by mentors, is a practice which has been implemented by many schools and colleges. Workforce reform has provided the resource for teachers to work in partnership with a learning mentor in identifying and responding to the learning needs of the individual. Supported by technology and a flexible curriculum delivered in a modular timetable, learners are encouraged to develop in a way that meets their needs (Blandford, 1991b). Social interaction with peers takes place in group work through the extended curriculum. Such scenarios are commonplace in Pathfinder and early adopter schools (Street, 2005). They can also be found among the learning networks commissioned and monitored by LEAs and children trusts. Consider:

1. How does your school respond to the needs of the individual learner?
2. Do you have a flexible curriculum and timetable?
3. How are vocational and academic needs identified and met?
4. Are all staff trained to respond to these changes?

Summary

To be a master in your class was the reason for the introduction of the Masters qualification; those who gained the award were recognised for their ability to teach their peers. Today, as a leading professional, a pedagogue is responsible for the development for the whole child which requires knowledge and understanding, skills and abilities to function in classrooms within a global community.

Questions for discussion

Consider:

1. How safe is the environment in which you teach?
2. How can you guide the learner as an individual within your classroom?
3. Is there a sense of progression for all learners?

The range of pupils in every phase of education is as diverse as their behaviour. Consider:

4. How does your behaviour policy relate to the individuals within your classroom?
5. Do all learners feel safe? Are expectations shared?
6. How do you communicate with your pupils?
7. Do you focus on behaviour for learning?

Teachers can find it difficult to manage their time effectively. To function effectively teachers need to be fit and healthy. Consider:

8. What interests do you have beyond teaching?
9. How do you ring-fence your spare time?
10. How relaxed are you at the start of the week/term?
11. What professional development activities do you engage in weekly, half-termly, termly, annually?
12. Are you a self-managed networker who learns from others?
13. What qualifications have you gained, or do you plan to begin studying, for post-initial training?
14. What will be the next professionally-related book you will read?

Coda: Can you swim?

References

Anno, M. (1986) *All in a Day*. London: Hamish Hamilton.

Blandford, S. (1991a) 'Arts and the Environment', in *Remnants*. London: English Heritage.

Blandford, S. (1991b) *Modular Curriculum*. London: Centre for the Study of Comprehensive Schools.

Blandford, S. (1997a) *Middle Management in Schools*. London: Pitman.

Blandford, S. (1997b) *Resource Management in Schools*. London: Pitman.

Blandford, S. (1998) *Managing Discipline in Schools*. London: Routledge.

Blandford, S. (2000) *Managing Professional Development in Schools*. London: Routledge.

Blandford, S. (2004a) *Professional Development in Schools Manual* (3rd edn). London: Financial Times Management.

Blandford, S. (2004b) *School Discipline Manual*. London: Pearson Management.

Blandford, S. (2005a) *Middle Management in Schools* (2nd ed). London: Pearson Management.

Blandford, S. (2005b) *Remodelling the Workforce*. London: Pearson Management.

Blandford, S. and Blackburn, N. (2004) *Financial Management in Schools*. London: Optimus.

Blandford, S. and Duarte, S.J. (2004) 'Inclusion in the community: a study of community music centres in England and Portugal, focusing on the development of musical and social skills within each centre', *Westminster Studies in Education*, vol. 27, No. 1, p. 97.

Blandford, S. and Shaw, M. (2001) *Managing International Schools*. London: Routledge Falmer.

Blandford, S. and Welton, J. (1999) *Restructuring: The Key to Effective School Management.* London: Routledge.

Carter, D. (2004) *The Key to Future Innovation.* Nottingham: National College of School Leadership.

Dahl, R. (1988) *Matilda.* London: Penguin.

Department for Education (DfE) (1994) *Code of Practice on the Identification and Assessment of Special Educational Needs.* London: HMSO.

Department for Education and Skills (DfES) (2001) *Special Educational Needs Code of Practice.* Nottingham: DfES Publications.

Department for Education and Skills (DfES) (2002) *Transforming School Workforce Pathfinder Project.* London: DfES Publications.

Department for Education and Skills (DfES) (2003a) *School Teachers Pay and Conditions.* London: DfES Publications.

Department of Education and Skills (DfES) (2003b) *Changes: Administrative and Clerical Tasks.* London: HMSO.

Department for Education and Skills (DfES) (2003c) *Raising Standards and Tackling Workload: A National Agreement.* London: HMSO.

Department for Education and Skills (DfES) (2003d) *The Future of Higher Education.* London: HMSO.

Department for Education and Skills (DfES) (2004a) *Removing Barriers to Achievement: The Government's Strategy for SEN.* Nottingham: DfES Publications.

Department for Education and Skills (DfES) (2004b) *Every Child Matters: Change for Children in Schools.* London: DfES Publications.

Department for Education and Skills (DfES) (2004c) *The Management of SEN Expenditure (LEA/0149/2004).* London: DfES Publications.

Department for Education and Skills (DfES) (2004d) *Five Year Strategy for Children and Learners.* London: DfES Publications.

Department for Education and Skills (DfES) (2004e) *Putting the World into World-Class Education.* London: DfES Publications.

Department for Education and Skills (DfES) (2004f) *Barriers to Inclusion.* London: HMSO.

Gibson, S. and Blandford, S. (2005) *Special Educational Needs Management in Schools*. London: Sage.

Guaspari, R. (1999) *Music of the Hear*. New York: Hyperion.

Gunter, H., Rayner, S., Thomas, H., Fielding, A., Butts, G. and Lance, A. (2005) 'Remodelling the school workforce: developing perspectives on headteacher workload', *Management in Education*, Vol. 18, no. 3, pp. 6–11.

Hayes, D. (2004) *Debates in Education*. London: Routledge Falmer.

Hughs, S. (2004) *Subject Leaders: Resource Management*. London: Optimus.

OfSTED (2004a) *Special Educational Needs (SEN) and Disability: Towards Inclusive Schools*. London: OfSTED.

OfSTED (2004b) *Provision of Music Services in 15 Local Education Authorities*. HMI 2296. October.

Powell, S. and Tod, J. (2004) *A Systematic Review of How Theories Explain Learning Behaviour in School Contexts?* London: Institute of Education.

Street, P. (2005) *Extended and Full-Service Extended Schools*. Extended and Full Service Schools Conference, 17 March, London.

TES (2005) 'What is education for? Part one: the future', *TES Supplement,* 21 January.

The Teacher (2005) 'That work life balance: the law and you', *The Teacher*, February, p. 36.

Thomas, A. and McNulty, T. (2004) *Remodelling the School Workforce*. Nottingham: National College of School Leadership.

Vygotsky, L.S. (1962), *Thought and Language*. Ed and trans. E. Hanfmann and G. Vakar. Cambridge, MA: MIT Press.

Warnock, M. (1978) *Report of the Committee of Enquiry into Education of Handicapped Children and Young People* (The Warnock Report). London: HMSO.

Index

accountability 22–3
All in a Day 28
allocation models, budget management 33
Anno, Mitsumasa 28
anti-crisp outburst 7
arts 64–74
    creative ideas 72–3
    school performances 70–1
    student performers 68–9
assessment 55–7
see also public examination system

Back to the Future 90
behaviour
boundaries of acceptable 46
    modification 42
    positive reinforcement 41–3
    rewards and praise 47–9
    see also misbehaviour
budget holders, teachers as 32–4
buildings, learning environment 5

career routes, teaching 90–1
chairing, meetings 31
change management 87
classroom environment 37–9
classroom practice 36–63
    assessment 55–7
    behaviour
        expert help 51–3
        positive reinforcement 41–3
    communication 49–51
    environment 37–9
    focusing on individual ability 53–5
    public examination system 59–61
    referees 45–7
    report writing 57–9
    rewards and praise 47–9

scaffolding 39–41
stress and teacher effectiveness 61–3
successful teachers 43–5
Code for Success 15
collaboration 21, 28–30
collaborative model, leadership 34
communication 49–51
community
    schools as microcosm of 12–14
    sense of 6
community of learners, looking after the
    individual 1–3
compulsory training days 96
computers, limited impact on learning
    92–3
continuing professional development 82–3
Corsham Music Centre 65–7
creative ideas 72–3
crisp policies 7–8
curriculum
    geared to individual needs 98–9
    see also National Curriculum

Dahl, Roald 57
differentiation 53
discipline 46
distraction 18–20
duty of care 79

education, issues in 6–20
education policies 6
Education Reform Act (1988) 21, 22
educational provision 13, 88–9
effectiveness 9
expert help, bad behaviour 51–3

financial management, success in 32–3
financial statements, comparisons of 33

formal meetings 31
forming, team development 26
foundation degrees 84
Freire, Paulo 9
funding, devolution to schools 22
further education 84–5
further educational colleges, educational
        provision 88–9
'Futures' agenda 6, 87–101

global context, teaching 34
good practice 14–16

head teachers 22, 23
healthy snacks 7–8
Hughes, Simon 32

ideas, creative 72–3
inclusion 6, 8–10
individual needs
    giving priority to 22–4
    new curriculum geared to 98–9
individuals, looking after 1–3
induction, new qualified teachers 78–9
Inset 80–1
International Music Centre, Lisbon 65–7

joined-up thinking, lack of 6

leaders
    duty of care 79
    teachers as 24–6
leadership 21–35
    budget management 32–4
    collaboration 21, 28–30
    individual needs 22–4
    meetings 30–2
    teachers as managers and leaders 24–6
    teamwork 26–8
learners see community of learners
Learning for the 21st Century 29
learning
    limited impact of computers 92–3
    scaffolding 39–41
learning assistants, courses for 84–5
learning environments 3–5
lecturers, further education 89

Lisbon International Music Centre 65–7
local management, of schools 22

Management for Subject Leaders 32
managers, teachers as 24–6
Matilda 57
Maxwell-Davies, Sir Peter 98, 99
meetings 21–2, 30–2
mentors 75–7
misbehaviour
    expert help 51–3
    teachers as contributors to 36
    see also behaviour
Morris, Estelle 16
music, social importance 99
music centres, LEA–run 66

National Curriculum 22, 94–5
negative reinforcers 42
newly qualified teachers, induction 78–9
noise control 18–20
norming, team development 26

obesity 7
objectives 17
OFSTED
    report on music tuition 64, 66
    SEN report 10

personal safety 36
planning
    importance of 16–18
    staff training days 80–1
plans, unintended outcome of 17
policy overload 20
positive reinforcement 41–3
praise 47–9
professional development 75–86
    further study 84–5
    induction, newly qualified teachers
        78–9
    mentors 75–7
    provision for continuing 82–3
    staff training days 80–1
*Professional Development in Schools
    Manual* 84
public examination system 59–61
public private initiatives 1

punishment 42
pupils
    focusing on individual abilities 53–5
    making performers out of 68–9
    see also teacher-pupil communication;
        teacher-pupil interaction

recruitment, into teaching 90–1
referees, in the classroom 45–7
report writing 57–9
rewards 42, 47–9

scaffolding 39–41
school culture, meeting culture and style
        30–1
school management, culture of 25
school performances 70–1
schools
    educational provision 88
    local management of 22
    as microcosm of local community 12–14
    similarities with pantomimes 24–6
secretaries, role in meetings 31
self-confidence, development of 43
self-control 42, 46
self-esteem, development of 43
SENCO's, giving support 10–12
shouting 50
social provision 13
*Special Educational Needs and Disability:
    Towards Inclusive Schools*
    OFSTED) 10
staff training days, planning 80–1
storming, team development 26
stress, teacher effectiveness 61–3
students, further education 89
successful teachers 43–5

successful teams 27

teacher-pupil communication 49–51
teacher-pupil interaction, and behaviour 42
teachers
    budget holders 32–4
    as contributors to bad behaviour 36
    as cultural negotiators 34
    focusing on what each pupil can do 53–5
    as managers and leaders 24–6
    need for collaboration 28–30
    role, encouraging good behaviour 42
    stress and lack of effectiveness 61–3
    successful 43–5
    unlocking the enthusiasm of learners 2
    see also newly qualified teachers;
        trainee teachers
teaching
    assessment to improve 55–7
    global context 34
    good practice 14–16
    recruitment 90–1
teaching assistants, courses for 84
Teaching Awards (2003) 90
team development, stages 26–7
teamwork, effective leadership 26–8
timetabling 3–4
toilets 38
trainee teachers, mentors for 75–7
training, for leadership 25
training days
    compulsory 96
    planning 80–1

Warnock Report (1978) 8
workforce remodelling 96–8